9-24-76

THE THEORY OF
RELIGIOUS LIBERTY IN ENGLAND
1603–39

The Thirlwall Prize Essay

1937

The Theory of
Religious Liberty in England
1603–39

by

T. LYON, B.A.

Sometime Scholar of King's College
Assistant Master at Eton College

"La fausseté doit-elle être combattue par
d'autres armes que par celles de la vérité?
Combattre des erreurs à coup de bâton, n'est-
ce pas la même absurdité que de se battre
contre des bastions avec des harangues et des
syllogismes?"

BAYLE, *Commentaire Philosophique*,
part II, chap. V

OCTAGON BOOKS

A DIVISION OF FARRAR, STRAUS AND GIROUX

New York   1976

Originally published by Cambridge University Press in 1937

Reprinted 1976
by special permission of the Financial Board, The Old Schools,
University of Cambridge

OCTAGON BOOKS
A DIVISION OF FARRAR, STRAUS & GIROUX, INC.
19 Union Square West
New York, N.Y. 10003

Manufactured by Braun-Brumfield, Inc.
Ann Arbor, Michigan
Printed in the United States of America

1942823

CONTENTS

PREFACE

THERE are three things about the nature and form of this essay which should be made clear. First, the limitation of the scope of the essay to the years 1603–39 is not an arbitrary division, but arises from the fact that it is during these years that the idea of religious liberty in England is first fully formulated. Secondly, it is upon this birth of the idea of religious liberty that I have concentrated the thesis of my essay. I have given incidentally a survey of the views of all sects in England on the subject of toleration, but with certain necessary limitations. Pressure of space has compelled me to omit the theory of the American colonists, which is in many ways intimately connected with the theory of the strictly English writers, and I have not included in my survey any writers who merely taught and did not publish during this period. This is a regrettable necessity, but American theory—leading as it did to the establishment of the first really tolerant states of the modern world—is in reality only a development and an adaptation to different conditions of a theory which was first born in England, and can therefore be omitted without seriously amputating the development of my general thesis. As for theorists who taught but did not publish during this period, it will in all cases be found that their historical position in the development of the idea of religious liberty is in the years of their publications. Jeremy Taylor, for example, taught during the years at present under consideration, but it would be absurd to consider his theory save under a survey of the general debate on toleration which succeeded the summoning of Parliament in 1640. No such general debate took place earlier. Thirdly, I have chosen to present my thesis by an analysis of the views of different religious parties. This may, perhaps, obscure slightly the chronological events of my period, but it is an assistance in the exposition of the theoretical development with which I am most concerned. Ideas never develop in the strictly chronological way that events must, and the development of the idea of toleration will be found to be a development by sects, not strictly and minutely in the logic of time. Nevertheless, a broad and general chronological development there is, and this I have endeavoured to indicate.

Since this essay was written the second volume of Mr W. K. Jordan's *Development of Religious Toleration in England*, covering the period 1603–40, has been published. Of Mr Jordan's first volume covering the Tudor period I have made extensive use, and indeed it was this work which first interested me in the idea of religious liberty in England. But with the exception of one or two minor additions, the research upon which this book is based was done before Mr Jordan's second volume was published. Mr Jordan's work is a history of the practice of toleration as well as of the theory. This essay is specifically directed to the study of the birth of the idea of religious liberty in England, and has therefore more of a connected thesis than Mr Jordan's extensive survey.

PREFACE

I have differed from Mr Jordan on certain points. Differences from his first volume are indicated in chapter II. Differences from his second are not indicated in the text, but consist mainly in my treatment of Barrowist theory as differing in some slight, but theoretically important, degree from that of the Congregational Independents.

I am indebted to Mr M. L. Clarke for assistance with the proofs.

T. L.

1937

CHAPTER I

INTRODUCTORY

WHEN COLERIDGE divided human beings into Platonists and Aristotelians he was aiming at an important truth which has many implications. Realists and Nominalists, Intuitionists and Empiricists, Idealists and Utilitarians, represent different forms of a fundamental antithesis which runs through all philosophy and therefore through human nature itself. Coleridge's dictum has all the untruth of a generalization in it, of course, but provided we limit its function to a distinction between methods of approach to intellectual problems, and to the general nature of the conceptions thence derived, we shall not be pressing it beyond the bounds of truth into falsehood.

One has to read but little in the literature of the idea of toleration to appreciate that tolerationists can likewise be divided into two sorts. They are united in their common concern with toleration and freedom of thought,[1]

---

[1] It will be noticed that "toleration" and "freedom of thought" are here used as almost identical terms. There is, of course, an important distinction between them, but in most senses the two present the same problem. It is true, as Mirabeau said to the French Assembly in 1789, that if one considers "la liberté la plus illimitée de la religion, un droit sacré", one is bound to consider "le mot tolérance qui voudrait l'exprimer", as "en quelque sort tyrannique lui-même, puisque l'autorité qui tolère, pourrait ne pas tolérer". But if toleration is not absolute freedom of thought, yet it is the nearest to absolute freedom to which human society is likely to approach. In any state there must be some criterion of what is and

and to both of them the problem of how a man shall be justified is of paramount importance. But in their methods of approach to toleration, and in the nature of the conclusions thence derived they differ as fundamentally as Coleridge's Platonists and Aristotelians. The first sort of tolerationists are those whose lives are conditioned by the passionate conviction that they are in possession of known and ascertained truth—not truth valid for themselves alone, but true for all men at all times and in all places. In the acceptance of this absolute truth lies the justification and salvation of man, both in the eyes of God, and of his fellow creatures, and without it there remains only eternal perdition. For them the kingdom of heaven has not many gates, but only one, and that narrow, and admission thereto, although in part by a moral life, is much rather by the intellectual acceptance of a creed which postulates certain beliefs concerning the nature of the universe. The belief of these thinkers, therefore, in toleration is in some sense incidental to their main preoccupation in life. They may be tolerant from a conviction which is a corollary to their creed (the early Anabaptists are a good example of these), or they may be a persecuted sect who have had a belief in tolerance impressed upon them by the force of circumstances. But to both toleration is not an end, but a means to the great light, and one feels that they would be prepared to abandon tolerance, could they

what is not expedient, and upon not offending this criterion freedom of thought must in practice depend. There is no greater imperative to human society than its own preservation. We must live before we can think, and there is no tyranny so oppressive as the tyranny of anarchy.

find a quicker means of getting there. Their belief in toleration thus springs rather from a dislike of persecution than from any positive faith in tolerance as the only way to truth. Their passionate faith in a particular truth, moreover, makes these thinkers fanatics. Whatever their intellectual faith they are temperamentally intolerant, and breed intolerance in others. The pursuit of freedom with an intolerant mentality may be self-defeating. The *Areopagitica* of John Milton is the most inspiring of all defences of liberty because it is the product of a mind passionately convinced of a particular truth, which yet realizes that toleration is the only way to it. But "for all his imagination, learning and literary magnificence in defence of freedom, the example of Milton's life probably does as much to retard the cause as to advance it".[1] It should not be forgotten that if Milton pleaded to be given "the liberty to know, to utter, and to argue freely according to conscience above all liberties", he also wrote a sonnet which began

Avenge, O Lord, thy slaughtered saints, whose bones
Lie scattered on the Alpine mountains cold.

The great merit of this first sort of tolerationist, however, is that his ideas on the means and methods of toleration tend to be detailed and explicit. Being usually of a persecuted sect his plea is intended less to make men reasonable, than to secure his own and other consciences against violation by civil force, and he is therefore forced not infrequently to consider the relations between, and the respective spheres of, Church and State, and how

[1] Whitehead, A. N., *Adventures of Ideas*, p. 66.

3

toleration can be secured at any given moment. But notwithstanding their practicality of means, the toleration of these thinkers is a moral rather than an intellectual triumph. Their conception of saving truth being absolute and narrow, they tolerate differences rather from charity to error, than from any positive belief in toleration and freedom of thought as the only possible means whereby the individual may find a saving truth for himself.

The second sort of tolerationists are those in whose life no great light shines, but who light the darkness of the way by their own reason and intelligence. These are they who are sceptical about human beliefs being efficacious towards salvation *per se*, and who emphasize that the justification of man is as much moral as intellectual. For them truth is not so absolute, still less so ascertained, that a man should be damned for an error which he sincerely believes to be true. Most of them believe in some absolute fundamental truths—but these are few, simple, and apparent (as simple faith in God and Christ to the Christian). All other beliefs can be but relatively true, and the justification of a man lies, therefore, largely in the honesty and sincerity with which his beliefs are held. The problem of where truth lies is, for these thinkers, no easy one to answer, and therefore their belief in toleration is something more than a mere negative dislike of persecution. They have a positive faith in reason, and in the methods of reason, for without liberty to follow the logical processes of the mind a man may be forced into dishonesty—intellectual dishonesty—and insincerity. To them, therefore, toleration is no mere corollary to a creed, but of direct and immediate importance, since it is the foundation of their whole attitude to life.

Being, however, latitudinarians, and rarely of a persecuted sect, the ideas of these thinkers on the methods and means of toleration are frequently less detailed and explicit than those which the pressure of circumstances have forced others to consider. There is no immediate necessity for them, as individuals, to consider the relation between Church and State, and their pleas for toleration are less solutions to the problems of persecution at any given moment than general pleas that men should behave according to reason, and avoid the futilities of fanaticism. But if they have no solution, other than this, for the immediate problems of the moment, they do have the supreme merit of being temperamentally tolerant and of inducing tolerance in others. Erasmus was the embodiment of rational tolerance in an age of fierce fanaticism, though his statements on the subject are far less explicit and uncompromising than those which Luther preached but rarely carried out. Montaigne was tolerant in his conduct and has induced many to follow his example, but there are few statements on toleration in the *Essais* —and certainly far less explicit than those of the German Anabaptists. It is through his own reasonableness and suggestive scepticism that Montaigne's influence in the cause of tolerance has been invaluable. Voltaire again—the very apostle of reason and tolerance in life—has written a *Traité sur la Tolérance* which is negligible compared with, say, the weightier work of

5

Bayle,[1] who was forced into exile in Holland. But Voltaire's services in the cause of tolerance are no less important than those of Bayle. For the truth is, toleration to this second sort of tolerationists is an intellectual rather than a moral triumph. It has been seen that to the first sort of tolerationists the justification of a man lies in the acceptance of a creed which postulates certain beliefs concerning the nature of the universe. In other words, the justification of a man is for them in some sort intellectual, and tolerance a moral triumph of truth showing charity to error. With the second sort of tolerationists the position is exactly reversed. Justification for them is moral—the honesty and sincerity with which a man holds his beliefs, and toleration thus becomes an intellectual triumph, for only by the free use of the logical faculties, of reason, can a man find out what he honestly and sincerely believes to be true.

In his *Religious Liberty*—a book much praised by Bury—Francesco Ruffini makes this distinction between the two sorts of tolerationists the explanation of the two different systems by which toleration has in practice been secured in modern states. The first sort of tolerationist, those who in general are the descendants and successors of the Anabaptist movement, have invariably advocated a system of rigid separatism, that is to say of disallowing to the State any right or power whatsoever of interference in religious or ecclesiastical affairs. They insist upon the separation of Church and State. It is

[1] *Commentaire philosophique sur ces paroles de Jésus-Christ "contrains-les d'entrer"*.

6

true that had the State shown itself willing to adopt
another alternative—that "of bending itself supinely
before the Church, scrupulously modelling all its laws
and its every action upon the Church's dictates, and
affording the Church without question the support of
its material forces",[1] the political theory of these thinkers
might have developed along theocratic rather than
tolerant and separatist lines. Toleration was to them,
after all, only a means, and not an end. But this was an
alternative that the State was not willing to accept, and
it was thus that their political theory became one of
rigid separation. In practice their theories have received
considerable application. The United States of America
and the French Republic are both states in which
religious toleration is secured by a system of legal
separatism, and in which the State holds itself aloof, not
interfering in religious affairs, and recognizing its in-
competence in regard to them.

The second sort of tolerationists, the historical heirs
of the Socinians and the Confession of Rakau, developed
a very different political theory. It was their hope,
in the first place, that they would need no political
theory at all. Their plea was that men should behave
reasonably and avoid factious and fanatical conduct,
and it was in this that they saw the real solution to the
divisions and recriminatory persecutions of Christendom. But such advice fell upon deaf ears in the sixteenth
and seventeenth centuries as it has done in all centuries
before or since, so that these apostles of toleration
"found themselves under the necessity of seeking

[1] Ruffini, F., *Religious Liberty*, p. 497.

assistance and support for their propaganda of pacification in the sole power which was in a position to impose peace—that is to say, the State. And it is for this reason that, according to their teaching, the State cannot detach itself from ecclesiastical affairs, but must maintain and exercise its authority—the so-called jura circa sacra—over them, naturally not with the intention of favouring a particular religion or helping it to impose its supremacy on the others, but solely for the purpose of keeping all the religions in check, and of imposing upon all, willing and unwilling, the principle of universal tolerance and reciprocal respect. Substantially it was the same thought which urged Voltaire to recommend the maintenance of a state religion: 'Afin de réprimer les entreprises des fanatiques et les désordres qui en résultent.'"[1] When applied to actual states this system has received divers names according to the country in which it has been practised—Erastianism, Gallicanism, Josephism, Royalism, Jurisdictionalism, etc. Perhaps the best example of this jurisdictional system in practice is the religious system of Frederick the Great, and of successive Prussian legislators. It is not without significance that Frederick was counselled in these matters by Voltaire.

There is, however, one important consideration which Ruffini tends to overlook in his distinction between separatist and jurisdictional systems of legal religious toleration. It must not be forgotten that the end of both systems is religious liberty, and religious liberty must in practice mean the denial to force, which is usually

[1] Ruffini, F., *Religious Liberty*, p. 495.

concentrated in the State or civil authority, of any right to interfere with a person's beliefs. This denial of such a right to force may be either absolute or limited—it depends upon the degree of religious toleration that is established—but if any toleration is to be secured at all it must in practice involve the restriction of the right of those in possession of force to interfere with the religious beliefs of any single person. It is true, of course, as Ruffini points out,[1] that the religious liberty desired by the first sort of tolerationist may be very different from the religious liberty desired by the second. To the former it is much more ecclesiastical liberty that is desirable—that is to say, the liberty of particular churches or congregations to organize themselves as they will no matter how intolerant they may be within themselves—rather than that liberty of thought which seems desirable to latitudinarians. But, after all, both parties have "liberty", in whatever degree, in common, and liberty in practice can only be secured by denying any ethical purpose or function to the civil authority, or to any other authority possessed of force. Again, this denial may be either absolute—the refusal to allow the State any ethical purpose or function whatsoever—or partial, as for example, where the State is permitted to defend true religion by force, but not to force all men to it. Further, this denial of an ethical purpose and function to force may be secured, as we have seen, in two ways: by a system of legal separatism, where the denial of ethical and religious functions to the civil power is explicitly and legally recognized; or by a jurisdictional

[1] *Ibid.* pp. 497–9.

9

system where there is no such legal recognition, but where, in practice, the civil power does refrain from using powers which it claims legally to possess. But in all cases, if there is any toleration at all, the practical result must be the withdrawal of the civil authority, or any other authority possessed of force, from the control of certain spheres of human conduct. In other words, to all tolerationists, of whatever type, there is in common (which is perhaps obvious enough) a disbelief in the use of force in certain spheres of human conduct; and therefore, some measure, greater or less, of denial of an ethical or religious purpose to the sole authority which in practice controls the use of force—the State.

The distinction between these two types of tolerationist, and their respective political theories, is to some extent the distinction Troeltsch draws between the "church" type of Christian organization, and the "group" or "sect" type.[1] The former of these have interpreted the Gospel not literally and strictly, and have therefore accepted the world as it is, and, by compromising with it, have sought to transform it. Their social teaching has thus been on the whole that of accepting existing authority, and of rationalizing the Christian ethic in accordance with existing conditions, seeking meanwhile to Christianize them. The Roman Catholic Church accomplished this for the Middle Ages, and the philosophy of St Thomas saw Christendom as a society at once spiritual and temporal, in which every living person had his allotted task to fulfil towards the

[1] In *The Social Teaching of the Christian Churches.*

salvation of the whole, and in which nature, and the relative natural law of the fallen state, were transformed, by the power of redemption lodged in the Church, into super-nature and the state of grace. The Calvinist Church, which began by having marked affinities to the "group" type of Christianity, has in the end done for modern capitalist society what the Roman Church did for mediaeval. It has accepted existing authority and conditions, and in sanctifying them has sought to transform them. This "church" type of Christian organization has then very clear affinities to the second sort of tolerationist—the latitudinarians. And this, not only because the latitudinarians have nearly always belonged to the dominant "church" type of Christian organization, but also because, like the churches, they have accepted authority as it is, and have sought to change conditions by gradually making men more tolerant and reasonable, as the churches try to make them more Christian.

The "group" type of Christian organization has never, by its very nature, possessed the power, numbers or dominance of the churches. It has always adhered to the Gospel literally and strictly, and has therefore been led, not to accept the world, nor to compromise with it, but to renounce it and condemn it as wicked and sinful —the work of the flesh and the devil. The "groups" are less permanent and enduring organizations than the churches, and they tend to be sporadic and intermittent phenomena, occurring when sensitive religious consciences can no longer bear the complacency and compromise of the churches towards authorities and conditions which they come to deem little less than the works of the devil. This phenomenon has been visible in history from the time of the early ascetics (whom the Roman Church so skilfully organized into communities of monks and friars within the *corpus christianum*) to the great outburst of sects which succeeded the Protestant Reformation, and of which the Anabaptists are the most typical, and certainly, from the point of view of this dissertation, the most important. To these "groups", as to the first sort of tolerationist, there could be only two possible political theories—complete theocracy or rigid separatism, and as the State, as we have seen, was unwilling to accept the former, it was along separatist lines that their political theory developed.

It is, in part, the intention of this book to attempt to estimate the various contributions of latitudinarians and separatists to the idea of toleration in England during the years 1603–39. There are two reasons why this period is of especial interest.

The first reason is the nature of what Mr Basil Willey has called "the seventeenth-century background". The early seventeenth century was one of those periods in history in which men find the problem of truth and of their own justification more pressing and more acute than it was to their predecessors. It was not merely that in England great issues were at stake in Church and State, but also that there was considerable intellectual perplexity and disillusionment amongst all thinking men. The sixteenth century had in many ways been born with the hope of a new world—whether the Humanist world of the Renaissance, the Protestant world of the Reformers, or the Catholic world of the Counter-Reformation—but by the opening of the seventeenth century it had become clear that men were just as foolish, sinful, heretical as they had been before. Protestantism continued further to define and further to divide, and the number of exclusive and absolute ways to salvation was as great as the number of sects who propagated them. As Mr Willey has shown[1] the vast philosophic synthesis of the Schoolmen and St Thomas, which the Reformers and the Humanists had both rejected, had not as yet been replaced by another, and it was therefore not unnatural that there should be much intellectual confusion and uncertainty—an uncertainty which found expression in the quite remarkable number of "conversions" (from John Donne and William Chillingworth down to such undistinguished people as the Countess of Buckingham) to and from Catholicism —the embodiment of the older philosophic synthesis.[2] Donne's sonnet is perhaps not untypical of his age:

Show me, dear Christ, Thy spouse, so bright and clear.
What! is it She, which on the other shore
Goes richly painted? or which rob'd and tore
Laments and mourns in Germany and here?
Sleeps she a thousand, then peeps up one year?
Is she self-truth and errs? now new, now outwore?
Doth she, and did she, and shall she evermore
On one, on seven, or on no hill appear?
Dwells she with us, or like adventuring knights
First travel we to seek and then make Love?

[1] In *The Seventeenth-Century Background.*
[2] *Vide* Hallam, H., *Introduction to the Literature of Europe...*, II, 408.

Betray kind husband thy spouse to our sights,
And let mine amorous soul court thy mild Dove,
Who is most true and pleasing to thee, then,
When she is embrac'd, and open to most men.

In some sense the intellectual distress of the early
seventeenth century was similar to the *mal du siècle*
which afflicted the French Romantics after the French
Revolution had destroyed the dreams of the philosophers, or to the modern uncertainty which has ensued
on disillusionment with nineteenth-century liberalism.
The separatist and latitudinarian tolerationists agree in
regarding religious liberty as in part a solution to this
problem, but they approach a common idea by profoundly different ways.

In the second place the birth of explicit thought on
religious liberty, both separatist and latitudinarian,
occurred in England during the years 1603–39. It is
true that in the later years of Elizabeth there had been
separatist teaching from the Brownists and Barrowists,
and that Hooker was in some sense the first English
latitudinarian, but, as will be seen later from a precise
examination of the exact implications of the separation
of Church and State, it was not until the reign of James I
that any sect really arrived at the idea of complete and
absolute separatism, and appreciated fully the implications of religious liberty. The purely theological development of sects under James into extremer degrees of
separation from the Church of England is accompanied
by a progressive change in their interpretation of the
social implications of Christianity, and especially in
their views on the power of the magistrate in the

Church, which, in England at all events, was the most urgent politico-theological problem facing Christians in the late sixteenth and early seventeenth centuries. As their theological views became more extremely Protestant, so their views on politics became more nearly those of the group type of Christian organization, and approached more nearly the idea of religious liberty.

CHAPTER II

THE POSITION OF THE IDEA OF
TOLERATION IN 1603

THE Catholic theory of persecution had been formulated by St Augustine and related by St Thomas Aquinas to the great body of scholastic philosophy. Since the Church contains and controls the full body of truth, and without it there can be no salvation, St Thomas declared that heretics are worthy not merely of excommunication, but of exclusion from the earth by judicial death. For him errors in the faith constitute moral guilt, and though the Church should warn the heretic, if he persists, he must be relaxed to the secular tribunal for execution. If the violator of a civil law may be justly executed, it is incomparably more just to slay one who threatens the spiritual welfare of generations yet unborn. No one may be compelled to enter the Church—and therefore the Church has no power over Turks and Pagans—but once having entered its communion he must, if necessary, be forced by violent means to lend obedience to its faith.[1] That Aquinas should teach, and the Church practise, the relaxation of the heretic to the secular arm was not simply an attempt to cast the odium of persecution upon

---

[1] The whole of this chapter is indebted to Mr W. K. Jordan's *Development of Religious Toleration in England*, vol. I, of which it is in some sense a summary and a criticism.

the secular rather than the spiritual authority. Catholic theory consistently separated the spiritual sword from the temporal sword, though it would allow both to be used for a spiritual end. The spiritual sword was exercised by the Church and at her discretion; the temporal sword by the civil authority but still according to the Church's dictates.

The effect of the birth of modern capitalist and nationalist society, and of the two intellectual movements which accompanied it—the Renaissance and the Reformation—was to shatter irredeemably the social basis upon which the mediaeval theory of theological persecution had been found practicable. The Church was no longer the sole organized authority in Christendom, and though it was, of course, possible that the sovereign nation State might be so theocratically minded as to obey the dictates of the Pope, as some mediaeval emperors had done, yet in practice even Catholic states in sixteenth-century Europe did not hesitate to limit the power of the Pope where they found it convenient, and to put secular and political considerations before the preservation of the true doctrine.[1] It is true that the sovereign State may be even more intolerant than was the Catholic Church during the Middle Ages, but once persecution has become a wholly political question, the obstacles to toleration are far less, because it has then only to be demonstrated that persecution raises more political problems than it solves. The establishment of

[1] This was a favoured cry of Protestant pamphleteers in England, so much so that Cardinal Allen replied to it in his *Defence of English Catholics*.

international toleration, as at the Peace of Augsburg, on the basis of *cujus regio ejus religio*, is the first step to appreciating the benefits of toleration within the State. Experience of the political instability produced by the persecution of religious minorities will prove in time that toleration and not religious uniformity is essential to the safety of the State.

But it was the success of the Protestant revolt, and the rejection by both Humanists and Reformers of the philosophy of St Thomas, that finally put an end to the conditions under which the Catholic theory of persecution had been capable of universal application. With the exception of More's *Utopia*[1] the Renaissance made no direct and positive contribution to the idea of toleration, but it sowed the seeds of a rational scepticism without which the latitudinarian interpretation of the idea could not grow. From the first, however, Protestantism had within itself the germ of the idea of toleration. Not, of course, that it established liberty; but in a creed which preached justification by faith as opposed to justification by works, it was inevitable that sooner or later someone should point out (as Luther, indeed, did himself, though his practice and subsequent theory did much to belie it) that though a man can be forced to outward works and reception of the Church's ministrations, faith can be commanded by God alone. Moreover Protestantism was the first successful heresy, and as it continued to define its beliefs, and further to divide over them, the number of sects thereby created made some form of

[1] The tolerant passages of More's *Utopia* are quite unrelated to any subsequent development of the idea of toleration.

18

toleration inevitable, unless the holocaust of the sixteenth century was to continue indefinitely.

But all this is wisdom after the event; and the fact
remains that the sixteenth century was perhaps the
most intolerant century of European history. It was so
for this reason; that although the very existence of the
Reformers was a virtual denial of the theological theory
of persecution, yet in another form, the more powerful
Protestant Churches accepted that theory as implicitly
as the Catholic Church had done before them. Protestants, like Catholics, were still obsessed with the idea
of an absolute truth, entirely known, ascertained, and
definable, and it was difficult for them to believe that
men should not be forced to it. It is true that some of
the early statements of Luther urged a toleration and a
separation of civil and spiritual powers, and that Castell-
lion later in the century was able to quote a long list of
Protestant divines who had preached in favour of toleration,[1] but these were largely random statements whose
full implications the authors of them never really appreciated, and which never entered into the real logic of the
Lutheran or Calvinist positions. Luther, indeed, soon
came to appreciate the spiritual anarchy which would
ensue on some of his earlier pronouncements, and he
eventually became an Erastian in the strict sense of the
term; that is to say, he taught the divine right of the
godly prince, not to be absolute in the State, but to
govern the Church, to command for truth and to sup-

[1] In *Traité des Hérétiques* written under the pseudonym of
Martin Bellie. *Vide infra.*

press idolatry.[1] The Calvinist theory of theological persecution sprang from the belief that although the elect are known only to God, yet the earth must be made a fit abiding place for them—the ungodly disciplined in their interests.[2] Genevan intolerance culminated in the burning of Servetus, and the defence of the execution of heretics by Calvin[3] and Beza.[4] This was no mere political necessity manifesting itself in religious persecution: "mais bien la glaive civil mis à la disposition des haines théologiques; c'était l'intolérance d'un Pape, plutôt que celle d'un souverain; c'était en un mot l'intolérance d'une religion qui se révélait.... Avec Calvin la Réforme se montre non moins intolérante que le Catholicisme."[5] Acton would have said "more intolerant", because whereas Catholic theory justified persecution in defence of the Church, as in cases of apostasy, Protestant theory urged the persecution of all error and idolatry, Jewish and Pagan as well as Christian[6]. But the pure theological intolerance of Geneva was not the practice of all Protestant states, and the theory of the Reformers was well able to accommodate itself to the varying conditions of the states in which it had to be practised—as the diversity of Protestant

[1] For the appreciation of the importance of the godly prince theory in the sixteenth century, and the true meaning of Erastianism, I am indebted to an unpublished dissertation of Mr G. C. Morris. See also Lagarde, *Recherches sur l'esprit politique de la Réforme*, pp. 331–42.

[2] Tawney, *Religion and the Rise of Capitalism*, p. 117.

[3] In *Defensio Orthodoxae Fidei...ubi ostenditur haereticos jure gladii coercendos esse.*

[4] In *De Haereticis a civili magistratu puniendis.*

[5] Matagrin, *Histoire de la Tolérance Religieuse*, chap. III.

[6] *History of Freedom*, pp. 150–87.

theories on the right of resistance to princes shows. In general, however, sixteenth-century Europe did present the spectacle of the theoretical defence on theological grounds of much persecution which was actually inspired by wholly political motives.

Nowhere, perhaps, was this contrast more marked than in England. The English Reformation was perhaps the most political of all the religious changes of the sixteenth century. It was the hope of Elizabeth that ultimately her Church settlement might come to be accepted by the majority of Englishmen, and from the beginning the government (that is to say Elizabeth and her Council who, far more than the bishops, in practice controlled religious policy) disclaimed any desire to pry into men's consciences and private beliefs, provided only they would recognize that the Queen was Supreme Governor of the Church, and provided they would submit to an outward uniformity of religious worship.[1] Provided, in other words, they would submit to those conditions which were deemed essential to the security of the State.[2] Some persecution under Elizabeth was therefore inevitable, and the various penal laws against

[1] *Vide* Elizabeth, *Declaration of the Queen's Proceedings*.

[2] That such conditions were deemed essential to the security of the State was due to the fact that the maintenance of the Elizabethan government, and, indeed, of the throne of Elizabeth herself, came in practice to be identified with the maintenance of the Anglican Church. For all three were challenged on two sides: by Catholics, who, in seeking to restore the authority of the Pope, became involved in plots against the Queen's life, and in schemes for a Spanish invasion; and by Puritans, who, although their menace was more potential than real, were thought to be parity mongers in State as well as in Church. Elizabeth was clearly not to be re-

Catholics and Puritans testify to this. But it was a persecution which in practice was dictated by wholly political motives. With the exception of the execution of a few Anabaptists[1]—who were universally regarded with abhorrence as anarchists—no one was executed under Elizabeth without there was some political necessity, whether justified or not, dictating it. This is not to deny that many of the executed were martyrs to their faith. The respective allegiances of political duty and religious faith conflicted in some cases under Elizabeth, as they have frequently done before and since, and therefore he who was executed by the government as a traitor, might with equal justice be revered by his Church as a martyr to the faith. But the severity of the persecution invariably depended upon the degree of political danger.

It is impossible here to produce even a fraction of the evidence which Mr Jordan has adduced to show that the religious policy of the Elizabethan government, in so far as it was repressive, was motivated wholly by political considerations. The finest and fullest exposition of the governmental policy in this period is to be found in Burghley's *Execution of Justice in England for maintenance of Public and Christian Peace*; though the theoretical defence of it devolves rather upon Hooker.

assured by the Presbyterian policy of "tarrying for the magistrate", when Cartwright continued to teach that it was preferable that government in Church and State should resemble each other. *Vide* Pearson, A. F. S., *Church and State*: "Political aspects of Sixteenth-Century Puritanism", sect. 2.

[1] By 1583 there had been five executions in England for heresy since the beginning of Elizabeth's reign.

Hooker, like the framers of the Elizabethan Settlement, envisaged a broad church coextensive with the nation, because Church and State were for him merely two aspects of one body, and therefore Parliament could represent the people in religious as well as in secular matters. He insisted further[1] upon the necessity in any society of a unitary sovereignty, from which all jurisdiction, secular and ecclesiastical, must flow. "In politic societies there must be some unpunishable or else no man shall suffer punishment." The Puritans he therefore attacked as seeking to divide authority and impugn the Royal Supremacy. Hooker's importance to the idea of toleration is not merely his theoretical defence of the practical policy of the Elizabethan government, but also his advocacy of reason, which makes him in some ways, though he was far from advocating toleration, an anticipation of the latitudinarian tolerationists of the early seventeenth century.[2]

Nevertheless, it cannot be too strongly emphasized that behind these political motives there existed amongst Protestant divines in England a clearly formulated theory of theological persecution. This was quite a different rationalization of Elizabethan practice from Hooker's defence of sovereignty, though, as will be seen, Hooker himself was influenced by it.[3] All the divines

[1] *Ecclesiastical Polity*, book 8.
[2] *Vide* Buckle, *History of Civilization in England*, I, 310–40.
[3] It is natural that I should emphasize the importance of this theological theory of persecution in England more than Mr Jordan, because whereas he is concerned with the practical development of toleration, I am concerned more exclusively with the theory. Mr Jordan appreciates the widespread existence of this theory but

consistently held a theory of theological persecution. For them the Act of Supremacy was not a mere concession to State sovereignty or to political absolutism, and they disliked the frank avowal of the government that its religious policy was actuated by political motives. They sought, therefore, to justify both the Royal Supremacy and persecution on theological grounds. Even the government at times gave a theological justification of acts which were in fact inspired by political motives.[1]

The theological theory of persecution of the Anglican divines was essentially a Protestant theory of persecution, and was therefore neither mediaeval, nor was it held by the English Catholics. It was, in effect, the Lutheran theory of the godly prince, commanding for truth within his realms, and suppressing all idolatry and error. It was Erastian in the strict sense of the term, that is to say, it preached the divine right of the godly prince, not to be absolute in the State, but to govern the Church according to God's word, and to the truth which is plain and open to all men.[2] It differed from the Catholic theory of theological persecution, inasmuch as

[i]s inclined to underestimate its importance, especially when he refers to it as "mediaeval jargon", or when he writes that although "the views of Pilkington and Sandys and, on the whole, of the minor writers of the period evinced a growing disposition to justify the employment of rigorous repression in cases of dissent and misbelief" yet "Anglicanism did not venture to place the *raison d'être* for this policy higher than the requirements of ecclesiastical and political order", *op. cit.* p. 158.

[1] *Vide* Act against Bulls from Rome, 1571, 15 Eliz. c. 2.

[2] *Vide* Figgis, "Political Thought in the Sixteenth Century", *Cambridge Modern History*, III, 22.

the godly prince was no mere creature of the Church obeying its dictates with the temporal sword in spiritual matters, but was responsible to God alone for commanding that truth and suppressing that error which are apparent to all. The theory therefore presupposed that the Prince to whom it was applied was really godly, and also that truth was so known, and ascertained, that there was no real chance of the godly prince mistaking the truth in God's word. The scriptural sanctions for this theory were drawn wholly from the Old Testament, and its exponents were never weary of quoting the examples of Josiah and Hezekiah, etc., who were "nursing fathers" to the Church of Israel. This theory had been held in some form by all Anglican divines from the beginning of Elizabeth's reign.[1] But the most clear and explicit exposition of this theory is Thomas Bilson's *The true difference between Christian Subjection and Unchristian Rebellion*, which was published in 1585. That the absolutism which Bilson here attributed to the Prince in ecclesiastical matters did not extend to political affairs is clear from the permission he gives to a limited right of resistance to tyrants.[2] The power he gives,

[1] This Mr Jordan recognizes. Bishop Jewel, for example, the first Father of the Anglican Church, quoting the example of Solomon and David, asserts that it is the manifest duty of princes to drive sensual priests to their task and to protect the truth in the Church. Thereby, he continues, we grant no more power to magistrates than has been given them by the word of God, for a prince may understand religious and ecclesiastical as well as temporal causes. A king ought to be a patron and nurse of the Church, according to the example of Moses, Aaron, Joshua, David, Solomon, etc. *Apology for the Church of England*. Part. vi.

[2] Bilson, *op. cit.* part iii.

therefore, to the Prince in ecclesiastical affairs is not the result of a belief in State sovereignty, but of a theological theory of Church government, and hence, where it is repressive, a theological theory of persecution. Even Hooker, who, more than any other divine, defended the actual political practice of the Elizabethan government, mingles this theory of the godly prince with his defence of sovereignty in the eighth book of *Ecclesiastical Polity*—thereby weakening the theoretical strength of both theories. Because if the Prince has power in ecclesiastical affairs both as a godly prince and as sovereign, what is to happen if he acts in an ungodly manner? Is he to be obeyed as sovereign, or disobeyed passively as an ungodly prince? This was a problem that Hooker never really answered.

Now the importance of this theory is not merely that it is the theological justification of the Elizabethan Settlement, and that it explains why the bishops were content to allow the actual control of religious policy to the Queen, but also that, as a theory of theological persecution, it was the theoretical system with which those who were approaching the idea of toleration through separatism had to contend. The development of toleration in practice under Elizabeth, was due to the fact that the government, being actuated by political motives, was anxious not to persecute more than was politically necessary, and it was because any alternative to Elizabeth's government, whether Catholic or Puritan, would have been actuated by more theocratic motives than these, that the Elizabethan government was certainly the most tolerant government that England could then have had.[1] But as this practice was defended on theological grounds, so was it that with this theological justification impugners of it had to contend.[2] Moreover, this theory of the ecclesiastical power of the godly prince was in a greater or less degree accepted by all Protestant parties in England under Elizabeth, with the exception of the Anabaptists, who were practically non-existent.

The words "in a greater or less degree", however, are important, because it is by the degree of power which they attribute to the godly prince in ecclesiastical affairs that the various Protestant sects under Elizabeth approximate to the idea of toleration. No sect can be said to have arrived at the full idea of toleration, that is to say, the idea of toleration which implies religious liberty, but there were approximations to it, and statements of the case for a limited toleration, though often by implication rather than by explicit statement. No sect, in other words, was prepared to allow the magistrate absolutely no power over religious belief and practice. Some insisted on a strict separation of the executors of the spiritual and temporal powers, but these failed to distinguish between the ends for which these powers are to be used, and therefore never arrived at full separatism, while the latitudinarian conception never advanced beyond Hooker, who was almost its sole representative. But many Protestant thinkers did arrive at conceptions, which, had they realized their full

[1] Allen, J. W., *History of Political Thought in the Sixteenth Century.*

[2] The relations between the theory and practice of toleration will be considered at a later stage.

implications, or had they carried them to their logical conclusions, would have resulted in a theory of toleration. In the next few pages we shall consider the ideas of these Protestant sects.

The largest and most influential Protestant minority was the Puritans, whose ideas are represented by the Presbyterian system of Cartwright and Travers. Now the fact that the Puritans were a minority was of acute importance in the practical development of toleration, because they remained steadfastly uninfluenced by the governmental policy of comprehensive uniformity, and their very existence ensured a compromise, ending the insistence upon uniformity as essential to the safety of the State.[1] It was also fortunate because Puritan theory was highly intolerant. It is true that the Puritan insisted upon a stricter separation of Church and State than the Anglican—who, in the case of Hooker, regarded them merely as two aspects of one body, and, in the case of Bilson, as two means to one end. Cartwright denied that ministers may hold civil office, and regarded the Church as in every way a *societas perfecta*, complete, self-sufficient and free.[2] It is true also that the Puritan was devoted to the right of private judgment and was the first to defend the rights of conscience. But the Puritan was also entirely dominated by his belief in the divine right of the Presbyterian system, and therefore, although he was disposed to exclude the civil power from interference in spiritual affairs, as the result of his belief in the right of private judgment,[3] it was only from the spiritual

---

[1] Jordan, *op. cit.* p. 260.   [2] Pearson, *op. cit.*
[3] Jordan, *op. cit.* p. 261.

affairs of the true Church that he envisaged this exclusion. In all else the secular arm was viewed as the executor of religious policy, assisting the Church to discipline the ungodly in the interests of the elect. And the discipline was a severe one. The Puritan adhered more literally to Scripture than any other sect, and he derived thence not only a precise form of Church polity, rites and ceremonies, but in most cases a belief that the State was obligated by the judicial law of Moses, which included the death penalty for heresy.[1] Cartwright taught that if offenders against the first table of the Decalogue were punished with death, offenders against the second table would be less numerous.[2] The Church, moreover, as the moral instrument of God, should define and ferret out instances of evil and false worship, which the State under the guidance of the clergy should punish and exterminate.[3] Although, therefore, Cartwright asserted that the Prince is not head but only a member of the Church, and is subject to ecclesiastical censures, yet he also believed that the godly magistrate is a divinely ordained functionary whose privileges and prerogatives take the form of certain divinely appointed duties rather than rights.[4] The magistrate should procure godly reformation, and when it is secured, defend and preserve the true Church. He admits that the godly magistrate may in the last resort interfere even in the true Church to reform abuses. The Puritan theory of theological persecution, therefore, differed from the Anglican in the wider range of evils which it regarded as

[1] *Ibid.* p. 260.   [2] Pearson, *op. cit.* chap. v.
[3] Jordan, *op. cit.* p. 259.   [4] Pearson, *op. cit.* chap. ii.

worthy of punishment by the godly prince, and by the fact that the Prince is made much more, though by no means absolutely, the instrument of the Church. Both, however, agreed in preaching non-resistance and "tarrying for the magistrate" in case of an ungodly prince.

The most important contribution of the Separatists to the practice of toleration was the very fact of their separation, but, unlike the Puritans, they also made considerable advance in theory. Browne and Barrow were both influenced by the Church covenant idea of the Anabaptists, and they not only came to the belief in "reformation without tarrying for any"—that the true Church, which consists of independent congregations, must be erected with or without the magistrate's consent—but also to the conviction that the magistrate, by the nature of his power, was totally incompetent to erect a Christian Church.[1] The Anglican Church was for them sinful because it was not on a voluntary basis, and because "all the profane and wicked in the land are received into it" by the civil magistrate's decree.[2] Now had the Separatists been willing to apply these principles to all religious groups, irrespective of the nature of their religious truth, or had they even appreciated their logical implications in practice, they would have arrived at a full conception of toleration, implying religious liberty. But, although they denied the competence of the magistrate to erect a Christian Church, and therefore separated not merely the executors of the

[1] Jordan, *op. cit.* p. 264.
[2] Barrow at his trial, *Harl. Misc.* IV, 334.

two powers, but also made a partial separation of the ends for which they were to be used, both Browne and Barrow, and after them Francis Johnson[1], attributed power to the magistrate to suppress heresy and idolatry.[2] Separatists, as much as Puritans, were dominated by the idea of absolute truth, known and ascertained, and had they been in power they would doubtless have sought to impose their system on the nation. They would certainly have been more intolerant than the Elizabethan government was. Barrow, no less than Elizabeth, would have forced "all subjects to the hearing of God's word, in the public exercises of the Church".[3] In toleration for any other sect than themselves they were in most cases not interested. Nevertheless, they did render more important services to the idea of toleration under Elizabeth than any other sect. They were the first to separate systematically not only the executors of the two powers, but, in part, the ends for which they were to be used. Their insistence upon voluntary Churches consisting only of the regenerate and the elect, made it logically

[1] Particularly in *True Confession* of 1596.

[2] It is true that, in Browne's case, this power was only attributed to the magistrate in his later works (Letter to Mr Flower—published as *A New Year's Guift* by C. Burrage in 1904) and that Mr Jordan regards it as not having quite the weight of his earlier thought, because Browne was then returning to conformity. But this theory was so consistently held by all Congregational Separatists not only under Elizabeth, but in the early seventeenth century (though it is true that the seventeenth-century Congregationalists were the successors of Barrow rather than Browne) and was so much the accepted theory of the age, that Browne may even have held it before he openly declared so—contradicting, as it did, the logical implications of his other theories.

[3] Barrow, *Plain Refutation*, Preface quoted by Jordan.

impossible for the State to advance true religion by
weapons of intolerance, even though it might protect it
by suppressing idolatry, and therefore rejected the
primary error of persecution—that men can be forced
into salvation.[1] And under the pressure of persecution
towards the end of the reign, Penry and a few others
arrived at an idea of toleration (though, perhaps, it
would be more accurate to say "opposition to persecution") which comprehended other sects than their own,
and which urged that force cannot put down truth or
error.[2]

There was no systematic Baptist thought under
Elizabeth. English Baptism did not yet exist; though
the denunciation of persecution and of the use of physical
force in spiritual affairs by the two Flemish Baptists,
Pieters and Terwoort, who were executed for heresy by
Elizabeth,[3] was significant for the future.

The Protestant theory of the power of the godly
prince in ecclesiastical affairs, for which he was ultimately responsible to God alone, was not, of course,
shared by the Roman Catholics. These continued to
maintain their traditional theory, though the circumstances in which they were placed made it inopportune
for them to express it, but had they achieved power
there can be no doubt that it would have been put into

[1] Jordan, *op. cit.* p. 291.
[2] Penry, *Th' Appelation...unto the High Court of Parliament*;
Humble Petition of the Imprisoned Barrowists of 1593; both quoted
by Jordan.
[3] Jordan, however, quotes Froude's suggestion that Elizabeth's
real motive in allowing their execution was to flaunt, at a moment
that required it, her orthodoxy before Spain.

32

practice. Roman Catholics, however, could never agree that the Prince was responsible to God alone for his power in spiritual affairs, nor that he might force godly reformation on the Church without its consent, nor that the Prince might suppress non-Christian idolatry. For them the Prince had power in spiritual affairs only in so far as he obeyed implicitly the commands of the Church and the Pope, so that the difference between the theory of Catholics and Protestants might almost be reduced to this: that what the Protestant Prince did for God and at God's command as revealed in His word, the Catholic Prince did for the Pope at the Church's request. Although, however, Catholics made no real contribution to the idea of toleration, their position as a persecuted minority forced them to consider the question of toleration for themselves. To this the Jesuit party in England remained hostile, as they would be content with nothing less than supremacy, and they thought that toleration would diminish Catholic ardour, and compromise their cause. However, they were prepared to use all means to their end, and we therefore find them urging toleration of English Catholicism on grounds not dissimilar to the separatist pleas, at the same time as they were persuading the Pope that toleration would mean the ruin of the Catholic cause in England, supporting the political designs of Spain, and entering into treasonable conspiracies.[1] In their plea for the rights of conscience, especially by Parsons, the Jesuits were sincere, though it was only rightly informed Catholic conscience

---

[1] Jordan, *op. cit.* p. 373.

which should be free from persecution. The Secular party amongst the English Catholics not only requested toleration, but were prepared to compromise the Jesuit conception of Catholicism in order to obtain it. They denied the Pope's power to depose princes, and claimed to be concerned solely with religious matters, and not, as the Jesuits, with affairs of State. In some few cases they were even led to request toleration on grounds similar to the Politiques—that persecution is dangerous to the safety of the State.[1] As the Secular Catholics were the only religious party under Elizabeth to accept the government's contention that it persecuted only for political reasons, it is right that they should have given the logical reply to the governmental position.

Meanwhile, abroad, the Reformation had given birth to the full idea of religious toleration, comprehending all sects and creeds. The burning of Servetus had been the culmination of Protestant intolerance, and it provoked an immediate reaction. Even in the early days of the Reformation Zwingli had protested against the rigid doctrinal position that Protestantism, under Catholic pressure, was assuming. He taught that God might have his elect even amongst Gentiles, and that good men of all races might be saved, but Zwingli's views failed to influence the Protestant theory of the Church.[2] The *Traité des Hérétiques* of Sébastien Castellion, the *Satanae*

---

[1] See especially William Watson's *Important Considerations* of 1601.

[2] Jordan, *op. cit.* p. 329. It is significant that the best Anglican thought never adopted a theory of exclusive salvation, and that, through the Zurich exiles, the Anglican Church was greatly influenced by Zwingli.

Stratagemata of Jacopo Acontio,[1] and the *Dialogues* of Bernardino Ochino were the most distinguished expressions of later Protestant dissent from theological persecution and exclusive salvation, and they covered the whole range of toleration problems. Historically their ideas were almost as much indebted to the Humanist movement as to the Reformation. All three were profoundly influenced by the Italian Academicians, who themselves represented the reactions of Protestantism on the Renaissance.[2] The Italian Academicians, the "academic sceptics" as Calvin called them, presented a united front against bigotry and persecution; rejected the doctrine of the Trinity; and may be regarded as the founders of Unitarianism.[3] Following their expulsion from Italy, and then from Switzerland, they largely settled in Poland under Lelio Socinius, and later his nephew Faustus. Faustus spent the later years of his life in formulating the Socinian creed—the Confession of Rakau—one of the earliest confessions to embody full religious toleration. The Arminian movement in Holland, though it was not to be of decisive importance until the early seventeenth century, was an expression of dissent from the rigid Predestinarian doctrines of the

[1] Mr Jordan considers Acontius as an English lay tolerationist, on account of his residence for some years in England, and the dedication of his book to Elizabeth. But, as Mr Jordan agrees, his *Satanae Stratagemata* is not connected with the main trend of English thought on toleration, nor was it influenced by it. Acontius exercised little influence himself in England until the English translation of his work appeared in 1648, and it is much better to consider him as influenced by the Italian Academicians, for it was abroad that his thought was really formulated.

[2] Ruffini, *Religious Liberty*, p. 63.
[3] Jordan, *op. cit.* p. 306.

3-2

Calvinists, and as early as 1579 D. V. Koornhert and Jasper Koolhaes had both declared against persecution.[1] Before the end of the century the Socinians and the Arminians had come to embody liberal Protestant dissent from both persecution and doctrinal rigidity. All these thinkers and sects were essentially latitudinarians. They were agreed in condemning exclusive salvation and doctrinal rigidity, and desired to reduce the essentials to salvation to a minimum. Acontius had examined the psychological motives of persecution. Castellion had insisted that men were wasting their energies on doctrinal disputes to the neglect of morality and godly life.[2] The Socinians elevated reason to a higher position than any theologian had accorded it before. And the Arminians in Holland, where some measure of toleration for Protestants had been established, first exhibited the real political theory of the latitudinarian. They appealed to the magistrate to establish toleration by controlling all religious groups, and on this ground conceded him powers in ecclesiastical affairs. As early as 1579 there was a controversy at Leyden over the rival authorities of magistrate and ministers within the Church, in which the liberal theologians, headed by Jasper Koolhaes, supported the magistrates and argued toleration.[3] " Some time after, the ministers published an answer in the name of the Church to the Justification of the magistrates of Leyden in which among other things they said, That all other religions (besides their own) ought not to

---

[1] Harrison, A. W., *The Beginnings of Arminianism*, pp. 19–20.
[2] Buisson, F., *Sébastien Castellion*, I, 301.
[3] Harrison, *op. cit.* p. 20.

be tolerated, but rather forbidden and suppressed by the government, according to the examples of the Kings of Judah."[1] This clearly distinguishes the power which the latitudinarian tolerationist concedes to the magistrate for the purpose of maintaining toleration amongst many sects, from the power conceded him by those holding a doctrine of theological persecution for the purpose of maintaining one sect only. Nor was this latitudinarian movement confined to theologians. In France, where the religious wars had been more terrible than elsewhere, lay scepticism, not merely about exclusive salvation, but about religious salvation altogether, found expression in Rabelais and Montaigne, while the Politiques had concluded that toleration was essential to the very existence of the State.[2]

But the Reformation, uninfluenced by Renaissance liberalism, had also given birth to the separatist idea of toleration. The Anabaptists had carried the Protestant doctrine of justification by faith to its logical conclusion, and had rejected the baptism of infants for believers' baptism. They adhered strictly to the Gospel, believing that true religion resides in the inner light, and rejected all accretions later than the New Testament. From the beginning they had not only separated the executors of the two powers, and the ends for which they were to be used, but had adopted a wholly pacifist attitude towards the use of force, denying that magistracy could be lawful to a Christian, that the Christian had the *jus gladii*, that he might use arms, and even denying him the

[1] Brandt, *History of the Reformation in the Low Countries*, I, 370.
[2] Matagrin, *op. cit.* chap. III.

right forcibly to resist wrong.[1] The highest punishment a sinner was subject to was excommunication. The rising at Münster did, it is true, belie these theories, and attempt a theocracy by force, but the Münster rising was the result of severe persecution upon a few fanatics, who had thereby been deprived of their wiser leaders, and is not representative of Anabaptist theory (though, as has been seen, theocracy is one of the political alternatives open to this first type of tolerationist).[2] After Münster had fallen the harassed remnants of the Anabaptists were gathered together under Menno Simons who joined them in 1537. Menno and his followers expressly repudiated the distinctive social-revolutionary doctrines of the Münster Anabaptists and preached passive resistance. The taking of human life and of oaths were forbidden; and the magistracy and the army were both regarded as unlawful callings for a believer.[3] Menno preached widely in the Low Countries and Germany, but the most influential body of Mennonites were the Waterlanders settled at Amsterdam, by whom his name has been preserved.

The influence of both separatist and latitudinarian thought on the Continent was negligible in England under Elizabeth. There is little scepticism in English thought before the 1630's, and Anabaptism exercised no real influence on English separatism until 1609. But the concentration of Anabaptist separatism and Arminian

---

[1] *Vide* Anabaptist Articles printed for Swabians and Swiss near Schaffhausen in 1527 in McGlothlin, *Baptist Confessions of Faith*.

[2] Troeltsch, *The Social Teaching of the Christian Churches*, II, 704.

[3] *Vide* Mennonite Confession of 1580 in McGlothlin, *op. cit.*

and Socinian latitudinarianism in the Low Countries at the end of the sixteenth century was of immense importance for the future development of the idea of toleration in England, because it was in the Low Countries that exiled English Separatists were seeking an asylum. Moreover, since by 1603 the idea of toleration had proceeded as far as it could by implicit methods in England, and since the whole problem had been thoroughly debated explicitly abroad, it seems safe to assume that most educated men must have been aware of the existence of the idea, even if they immediately rejected it. Henceforward, therefore, we must look less for ideas which by logical process imply full toleration, than for explicit statements of the case for religious liberty.

CHAPTER III

THE ANGLICAN AND GOVERNMENTAL JUSTIFICATION OF PERSECUTION
1603–39

THE religious policy of the established Church and of the government during the years 1603–39 was largely controlled, during the reign of James, by the King himself, and during the reign of Charles by William Laud. Laud was not appointed Archbishop of Canterbury until 1633, but his influence was of growing importance from his appointment to the see of St Davids in 1621. It is, therefore, necessary to consider the two reigns separately.

During the reign of James the persecution of both Puritans and Catholics was motivated, as it had been under Elizabeth, by political considerations. But whereas under Elizabeth these political motives had been influential largely in persuading the government not to enforce the full rigour of the law, not to exercise in practice, unless it were politically necessary, the powers that in law it possessed, under James political motives led to an important development in the principle of toleration in law itself.

The motives and principles which guided James in practice are clearly expressed in his speech to his first Parliament in 1604.[1] Peace was always a main pre-

[1] Printed in Cobbett, *Parliamentary History*, I, 282.

occupation of James' life, and in 1619 he published a
tract called *The Peace-Maker*. This was a devotional and
moral tract, concerned largely with peace in private life,
and not mentioning at all the wider issues of toleration,
but in his speech of 1604 James considered peace in
relation to his foreign and domestic policy. After expressing his desire for peace abroad he turned to
consider civil peace. He began by opposing the Puritans
on the ground that "they are impatient of any superiority". But he had no desire to force any of his subjects
to his own opinions, "nay my mind was ever so free
from persecution or threatening of my subjects in
matters of conscience...that I was so far from increasing their burdens...as I have so much as either
time, occasion, or law could permit, lightened them".
Indeed, he desired "some overture" to be made to
Parliament to "clear those laws by reason" where they
had been "too rigorously extended". Roman Catholic
priests, however, could not be permitted to stay in the
kingdom as long as they maintained that the Pope had
civil power over kings, or that excommunicated sovereigns might be assassinated. As for the Roman
Catholic laity, though they would be free from persecution, they would not be allowed to win over converts to
their religion, lest their numbers should so increase as
to menace the liberties of the nation and the independ-
ence of the crown. At the Hampton Court Conference
James enlarged on his political reasons for repressing
Puritanism. A Scottish presbytery, he said, "agreeth as
well with a monarchy as God and the devil. Then Jack
and Tom, and Will and Dick shall meet and at their

pleasure censure me and my council and all our proceedings. Then Will shall stand up and say, 'It must be thus'; then Dick shall reply and say, 'Nay, marry, but we will have it thus'."[1] In reply to a Parliamentary Petition for the stricter enforcement of Acts against recusants in 1621 James adduced a further reason for not persecuting Papists more than was politically essential. The King refused "to make fresh laws against Recusants, because the present are rigorous enough, if enforced, and he is always urging other princes to moderation".[2] James feared that if the persecuting zeal of the Parliament was to have its way, Catholic princes abroad might retaliate upon Protestants.

James' policy towards the Roman Catholics in the latter half of the reign was largely conditioned by the negotiations over the Spanish marriage, an essential condition of which was that James should grant a toleration to the Papists. Despite the opposition from the Puritan Parliament, steps were taken, when the negotiations seemed likely to succeed, to establish this toleration in so far as it concerned matters of religion only; and in the summer of 1622 the Venetian Ambassador testified that "never was the Catholic religion more freely exercised in England".[3] On 2 August 1622, for example, John Williams, Bishop of Lincoln and Lord-Keeper, issued an order to the judges, at the instruction of the King, commanding a relaxation of the penal laws, and writs for the enlargement of Papists confined on any

[1] Barlow, "Sum of the Conference" in *The Phoenix Tracts*, vol. II.
[2] S.P. Dom. cxix, 103.
[3] Valaresso to the Doge Aug. 19 Venice MSS.

point of recusancy which concerns religion only and not matters of State. The reasons given for this order were "state reasons", and the hope that foreign princes might thereby be induced to favour Protestants.[1] The political nature of the motives influencing the King as much as the order itself produced an immediate outcry, because it was appreciated that the order was largely the result of the intrigues of Gondomar, the Spanish Ambassador, and of the King's desire to further the unpopular Spanish marriage.[2] In a letter to the Lord Viscount Annan, therefore, Williams defended the order, explaining that he is going to tell plainly his majesty's motives. Williams is forced to make concession to the intolerance of his opponents by his specious denial that it is a toleration, but he shows plainly enough the political motives of the King. His main defence is that contained in the order itself, that Protestants will only be tolerated abroad if Papists are shown some clemency here. He then proceeds to deny that it is a toleration, since a toleration looks to the future whereas the present indulgence merely condones past offences. Any future offenders will be committed, and will then be at the mercy of the King. If the Papists think that the favour is to their cause and not merely to their persons, and so should wax insolent, they will be reminded of their former estate. But most important, the writ is so framed as to "exclude many other crimes bearing among the Papists the name of recusancies, as using the function of a Roman priest, seducing the King's liege people from

[1] Lord-Keeper Williams to Judges, S.P. Dom. cxxxii, 84.
[2] Gardiner, *History of England*, 1603–42, IV, 349.

the religion established,[1] scandalizing or aspersing our King, Church, State, or present government. All which offences (being outward practices, and no secret motions of the conscience) are adjudged by the laws of England to be merely civil and political, and excluded by my letter from the benefit of those writs".[2] In other words, though James does not confess to his policy over the Spanish marriage, he asserts that his indulgence is wholly to matter of conscience, and that against those who are politically dangerous the law will remain in force as heretofore. Gondomar and the Catholics were not content with this, nor could they accept the thesis that outward practice was no matter of religion.

A year later the royal conscience was troubled over the taking of the oath confirming Charles' agreement with the Spaniards in Madrid whereby toleration was promised to the Papists who should come with the Infanta, and mitigation of the laws to English Roman Catholics. Lord-Keeper Williams was set the task of pacifying the royal conscience, and his advice to the King is therefore significant not only for his own views, but for the views he thought most likely to be found acceptable to the King. Two things appeared considerable to him in the matter. The first—the advancing of true religion—was a matter of conscience. The second—the suppression of adverse religion—admits of two degrees. Of these the first—"ita ut non praesit"—is likewise a matter of conscience; but the second—"ita ut

---

[1] We have seen in the speech of 1604 James' political reason for disallowing conversions.

[2] *Cabala*, I, 295.

44

non sit"—"His Highness dares not make this a matter of conscience and religion, but a matter of state only. If the Prince should make this a matter of conscience, he should not only conclude the French King to be a false Catholic, for not suppressing the Protestants; and the Estates of the Low Countries to be false Protestants for not suppressing the Papists at Amsterdam, Rotterdam, and Utrecht especially, but should conclude your sacred Majesty to have offended against your conscience... because your Papists are not suppressed, and your penal statutes have been so often intended and remitted. These things you may well do, this point continuing but a matter of state; but you may not do it without committing a vast sin if you now should strain it up to a matter of conscience and religion, against the opinion of all moderate divines and the practice of most states in Christendom." Williams concluded that the oath was neither against the conscience of the Prince, nor against his own, and the King was in conscience satisfied.[1] Williams' advice, of course, presupposes that the King holds a theory of theological persecution, and it will be seen later that this was indeed so. The words "dares not make this a matter of conscience" do imply that the King might, perhaps, like to; but even so Williams' advice is evidence of the political motives which were in fact controlling persecution and toleration, and it is the political argument that finally pacifies the royal conscience.

But this document is of further importance because it shows that the political approach to the question of

[1] Hacket, J., *Life of J. Williams*, p. 142.

45

persecution was, as far as toleration is concerned, bearing fruit. Williams is not obsessed with the inalienable right of truth to persecute error. His political approach has caused him to realize that there is a morality in these matters transcending the rights of the particular truths of Protestantism and Catholicism, and he appreciates that if it is a matter of conscience with the English King to extirpate all Catholics, it is as justifiable for the French King to make it a matter of conscience to extirpate all Protestants. James himself had none of the zealot's desire to persecute irrespective of consequences. In a speech to Parliament in 1624, replying to charges that he had neglected the established religion in the Spanish negotiations he said he always considered the interests of religion, but there were diverse ways of doing so. "It is true a skilful horseman doth not always use the spur; but sometimes the bridle and sometimes the spur; so a King that governs wisely is not bound to carry a rigorous hand over his subjects upon all occasions; but may sometimes slacken the bridle, yet so his hands be not laid off the reins."[1] In the negotiations between the King and the English Council, and the Lord-Deputy and the Irish Council over religious policy in Ireland at the beginning of the reign, there can be seen the policy of uniformity being mitigated by the practical difficulties which impeded it, and the governments on both sides of the Irish Sea learning by experience that force was not the most successful weapon with which to treat Irish Catholicism. On 4 July 1605 James issued a proclamation against

[1] Cobbett, *op. cit.* p. 1375.

46

toleration in Ireland, commanding all persons to repair to their several churches, and directing that all priests who remained in the country after 10 December should be banished.[1] Six months later the Lords of the Council, in certain instructions to Sir Arthur Chichester, the Lord-Deputy, were already concerned about the means whereby this policy was to be enforced. "To grant any toleration of that superstitious and seditious religion were greatly offensive to any meaning of his Majesty, were dangerous to the state and repugnant to good conscience. On the other side to enter directly on a compulsory course, while the multitude swayeth on the contrary part, might more weaken the cause by taking the foil, than bring present advantage (if it should not thoroughly prevail)." They advise a temperate course between these two, neither yielding any hope of toleration of their superstition nor startling the multitude by any general or rigorous compulsion. "Admonition, persuasion and instruction should be used before the severity of law and justice."[2] Chichester himself, who was asked by the Council to give reason for his rigour in forcing men to church,[3] and did so in a document typical of the attitude of shrewd politicians of his age— a mixture of political and theological justification[4]— wrote, at the same time, to the Earl of Salisbury a letter which shows that he also had learnt that force is not the

---

[1] *Irish Cal.* 1603–6, 513. *Vide* Gardiner, *op. cit.* I, 391.

[2] Lords of Council to Chichester. *Irish Cal.* 1603–6, 630.

[3] Lords of Council to Lord Deputy and Council of Ireland 3 July 1606. *Irish Cal.* 729.

[4] Lord Deputy and Council of Ireland to the Lords 1 Dec. 1606. Gardiner, *op. cit.* I, 397–8.

47

best weapon with which to treat conscience. "In these matters of bringing men to church I have dealt as tenderly as I might, knowing well that men's consciences must be won and persuaded by time, conference and instructions, which the aged here will hardly admit, and therefore our hopes must be in the education of youth; and yet we must labour daily otherwise all will turn to barbarous ignorance and contempt. I am not violent therein, albeit I wish reformation, and will study and endeavour it all I may, which I think sorts better with his Majesty's ends than to deal with violence and like a Puritan in this kind."[1]

But it was the substitution of the Oath of Allegiance in 1606 for the Oath of Supremacy as the test for Roman Catholics that constituted the most important contribution by James, inspired by political motives, to the principle of religious toleration. The Oath of Supremacy had required a denial of the spiritual as well as the temporal power of the Papacy within the realm,[2] and in law those who refused the oath on these grounds were subject to certain penalties, and therefore to persecution for their faith. Now Elizabeth rarely exercised this power in practice, and Burghley, in his *Execution of Justice in England*, had explained Elizabethan policy when he denied that Catholics who maintained the spiritual power of the Pope had been persecuted except for treason and disloyalty to the Queen. James now established in law, what Elizabeth had done in practice. The Act of 1606[3] does not ostensibly touch the Pope's

[1] Chichester to Salisbury. *Irish Cal.* 1606–8, 64.
[2] 1 Eliz. c. 1, sect. 7.   [3] 3 and 4 Jac. 1, c. iv, sect. 9.

spiritual authority at all.[1] It simply requires an oath of allegiance to the King which will hold whatever the Pope may decree. The Act was James' reply to Bellarmine's theory of the indirect temporal power of the Papacy. Bellarmine held that the Oath of Allegiance "non agi de sola civili obedientia, sed agi de fide Catholica, id est de primatu sedis Apostolicae, quem in scripturis sanctis apertissime fundatum Catholici omnes, ut fidei orthodoxae dogma certissimum habent".[2] This James denied, claiming that the oath touched no matter of religion and was concerned solely with civil obedience.[3] The oath was, indeed, James' definition of the respective spheres of Church and State in political practice, and although the views of Catholics and Anglicans, as to how far the respective spheres of Church and State extended, differed, yet, from the point of view of the separatist approach to toleration, it is a distinct advance on Hooker, who had regarded Church and State as two aspects of one body, and the Englishman as inevitably an Anglican.

Most of the political writings of James are concerned with proving that the oath does in fact treat only matters of civil obedience. In his *Apology for the Oath of Allegiance* he repudiates Bellarmine's charges, and asserts that the Cardinal has mistaken the Oath of Allegiance for the Oath of Supremacy.[4] In successive works[5]

[1] McIlwain, *Introduction to Political works of James I.*
[2] Bellarmine, *Responsio Mat. Torti ad librum inscriptum Triplici Nodo Triplex Cuneus*, p. 15.
[3] James I, *Triplici Nodo Triplex Cuneus*, 1607.   [4] *Ibid.*
[5] *A Catalogue of the Lyes of Tortus; A Premonition to all the most mighty Kings, Princes, in Christendom; A Remonstrance for the Right of Kings.*

he maintains this position against divers impugners of it, and denies that either Elizabeth or he ever persecuted save for treasonable offences. The clause in the oath, however, requiring Catholics to swear that the doctrine of the Papal power of deposition was heretical did much to belie James' assertion, since to require the condemnation of a doctrine as heretical, in addition to requiring that it shall not be carried out in practice, is clearly stepping beyond the bounds of civil obedience into problems of religious faith. In the *Premonition to all the most mighty Kings* James replied to this accusation. He expressly sought to prevent the Commons inserting such a clause, which in any case only asserts that, though the Pope may excommunicate princes, yet subjects are not thereby dissolved from their allegiance.

But if toleration in practice developed from the political approach to the question under James, in theory James held a doctrine of theological persecution, and with the Anglican Church of which he was Supreme Governor continued to assert the powers of the godly prince in matters of religion. Like most of his contemporaries James was still obsessed with the necessity for uniformity in Church and State, and it is this that constitutes the political justification of his persecution.[1]

---

[1] In the *True Law of Free Monarchies* (1598) James described monarchy as the most perfect form of government because "unity is the perfection of all things". In his *Basilikon Doron* of 1599 he refers to the Puritans as a factious discontented sect of parity-mongers likely to disturb "unity which is the mother of order" in both Church and State. And unity for James could only be achieved through uniformity.

But considering the powers in religious affairs that James ascribed to the Prince it seems probable that he valued the theological justification as well. In his speech at the opening of the Parliament of 1620,[1] as well as in his answer of 3 December 1621[2] to the Commons' Petition on Religion James admits that he "will never be weary to do all he can for the propagation of his religion and the repressing of popery", though this was admittedly a reply to a House of Commons more intolerant than he, which was rebuking him for his leniency. In the *Apology for the Oath of Allegiance*, however, despite the fact that he was denying persecution of conscience, James defines the powers of the prince in religious affairs. He brings proofs from Scripture to show that kings were the Lord's anointed and nursing fathers of the Church, contradicting Bellarmine's opinion which places them below bishops' chaplains. "If these examples, sentences, titles and prerogatives and innumerable others in the Old and New Testament, do not warrant Christian Kings, within their own dominions, to govern their church, as well as the rest of their people, in being custodes utriusque tabulae, not by making new articles of faith (which is the Pope's office) but by commanding obedience to be given to the word of God, by reforming the religion according to his prescribed will, by assisting the spiritual power with the temporal sword, by reforming of corruptions, by procuring due obedience to the Church, by judging and cutting off all frivolous questions and schisms, as Constantine did, and finally by making

[1] Cobbett, *op. cit.* p. 1173. [2] *Ibid.* p. 1338.

decorum to be observed in all different things for that purpose, which is the only intent of our oath of supremacy: If this office of a King, I say, do not agree with the power given him by God's word, let any indifferent man, void of passion judge." In the *Declaration* against Vorstius[1] James further declares "that it is one of the principal parts of that duty which appertains unto a Christian King to protect the true Church within his own dominions, and to extirpate heresies in a maximum without all controversy; in which respect those honourable titles of Custos et Vindex utriusque tabulae, keeper and avenger of both the tables of the law, and Nutritius Ecclesiae, nursing father of the Church, do rightly belong to every Emperor, King and Christian monarch". In the light of some of James' speeches to the Commons, the *Declaration* against Vorstius is a surprising piece of virulent theological intolerance. Conrad Vorstius was appointed in 1611 to the professorship of theology in the University of Leyden, but he held views concerning the nature of God which were certainly heretical, and which James described as Socinian. Vorstius presented no political menace to James; the States-General themselves were anxious to tolerate him; but James not only threw himself into the technicalities of the quarrel with all the zeal of a theological controversialist, he also brought diplomatic pressure to bear so that Vorstius might be dismissed his post.[2] In all the negotiations which constitute the *Declaration* James reveals himself

[1] James I, *A Declaration concerning the Proceedings with the States General of the United Provinces of the Low Countries in the cause of D. Conradus Vorstius.*

[2] Gardiner, *op. cit.* II, 128.

as having no appreciation whatsoever of the idea of toleration. He urges the States-General to "root out with speed those heresies and schisms which are beginning to bud forth amongst you",[1] and not to misuse the "liberty of your conscience", which it has cost them so much to win, by allowing the followers of Arminius, of whom Vorstius was one, to proclaim their wicked doctrines.[2] He urges not only the condemnation of Vorstius, than whom no heretic was ever more worthy to be burnt,[3] but the ending of "this licentious liberty of disputing and arguing unprofitable questions".[4] Later he admits that "it is not only tolerable but very commendable to propound questions or arguments, at leastwise in schools. But to devise new questions upon the principal articles of our faith, to enter not only into the secret cabinet of God, but to intrude ourselves into his essence" tends only to destruction.[5] Later James explicitly condemns toleration and liberty of conscience as dangerous. He rejects Vorstius' plea for the "particular man", with whom truth must begin, as dangerous to authority, and when Vorstius says that he is sure the King has no intention of imposing upon consciences, James replies that Vorstius is rejecting the judgment of authority in these matters. Christian liberty, for James, is applicable only to things indifferent, and to deliverance from the thraldom of the law and human traditions; not to introducing new doctrine into the world.[6] Liberty

---

1 Second letter of James to States in the *Declaration*.
2 The English Ambassador to the States, in the *Declaration*.
3 Second letter of James to States.
4 Letter to English Ambassador.
5 English Ambassador to the States.   6 *Ibid.*

of prophesying is a dangerous licentiousness causing schism and confusion in the Church.[1] A heresy over the nature of God, of course, does present the problem of toleration to a doctrinaire like James in an acute form; but it is hopeless to give a meagre recognition to the merits of disputation, to the right of reason freely to search for truth, and at the same time to assert that there are certain mysteries into which reason cannot pry. The year after these events had taken place James gave a demonstration of his orthodoxy at home, by the burning of Bartholomew Legate and Edward Wightman for Arianism. They were, however, the last heretics to be burnt on English soil.

The views of the Anglican Church on the power of the magistrate in the Church are best formulated in the canons which were drawn up in 1606. These were the official Anglican reply to the Jesuit attack on the Oath of Allegiance, and they argued a doctrine of complete non-resistance to the King in all causes, unless there should be express testimony of God of a new extraordinary prophet,[2] on the ground that obedience was due to the King actually in possession. It is true that James refused to sanction these canons because he believed that hereditary right was a better basis of authority than actual possession, but with the powers which the canons ascribed to the Prince he did not disagree. Canon 20 of Book I asserts that the kings in the Old Testament were charged by God to bring up their subjects in His fear, and that the institution of the

[1] Conclusion of the *Declaration*.
[2] Bishop Overall's *Convocation Book*, I, 25.

54

priesthood did not prejudice the King's authority in that behalf. Kings are bound to provide that their subjects have no false gods, are not idolatrous, nor blasphemous. Kings are bound by the law of grace as well as the law of nature to bring up their subjects in the true doctrine, and may consequently compel all their subjects, both clergy and laity, to obey their laws. Kings cannot, it is true, order priests to do as they list, but if they do priests must not withstand kings by force.[1] Canon 1 of Book II goes on to argue that these powers are not affected by the coming of Christ. Christ in no way weakened the obedience due to civil magistrates under the Law, since He came to fulfil the Law. Christ always submitted to the civil magistrate and counselled others to do so. In other words to the divine right of the godly prince in matters of religion there is now added the divine right of the Prince in matters of State, and Bilson's limited right of resistance to tyrants is disallowed.

Launcelot Andrewes, Bishop of Winchester, in his *Tortura Torti*[2]—a reply to Cardinal Bellarmine over the Oath of Allegiance, and the most considerable work in the whole controversy—further defines these powers conceded to the King in matters of religion. All the apologists for the oath agree in maintaining that it concerns mere matter of civil obedience. It does not require, as the Oath of Supremacy, a denial of the Pope's spiritual power. Nevertheless, though they were willing

---

[1] *Ibid.* I, 22.

[2] *Tortura Torti: sive ad Mat. Torti Librum responsio qui nuper editus contra Apologiam Serenissimi...Jacobi....Pro Juramento Fidelitatis*, 1609.

to make this concession in practice, in theory they retained their belief in the theological justification of the royal supremacy, and it is thus that Andrewes comes to ask what are the rights of the royal supremacy. Andrewes first defines what the royal supremacy does not imply. Under the name of the Supremacy the King does not bring into the Church a new papacy, that is to say he does not introduce into the Church either new articles of faith or new forms of divine worship. He does not handle holy things. He does not infringe on the office of priest. But there do belong to the King "ea quae exterioris sunt politiae", and by the law of God he is "custos et vindex non secundae modo tabulae, sed et primae". All men are ordered to be subject to him. Whatsoever the Kings of Israel did in religious matters, and did, not without commendation, that is his right and privilege. Amongst other rights, he may make laws concerning religion and enforce them, and though in so doing he should seek advice from those who are best advised in these things, he must also learn the law of God for himself. He may command the clergy as well as the laity, and even depose from the priesthood. He has power to regulate things indifferent, to set at rest profitless discussions, and to pull down false worship of all sorts. These rights of the royal supremacy are *jure divino*.[1]

Besides this theological justification of the power of the Prince in matters of religion, the controversy over the Oath of Allegiance also produced a justification

[1] *Tortura Torti*, p. 466 in the edition of the Library of Anglo-Catholic Theology.

almost exactly analogous to Hooker's. Like Hooker, John Donne approached in many ways the latitudinarian position. He is not such a champion of reason as Hooker, but his culture and breadth of mind give him a liberalism which is rare in early seventeenth-century theologians.[1] In his preface to *Pseudo-Martyr* Donne writes of his "easiness to afford a sweet and gentle interpretation to all professors of Christian Religion, if they shake not the foundation", and rebukes those "who . think presently that he hath no religion, who dares not call his religion by some newer name than Christian". Donne was not a believer in exclusive salvation,[2] and in Sermon 36 of the *Eighty Sermons* he urged the danger of bringing things disputed but not fundamental to over-vehement agitation. "Reproof", he writes, "is but a 'syllogismus', it is but an argument, it is but convincing, it is not destroying; it is not an Inquisition, a prison, a sword, an axe, an altar, or a fire." But this applies only to errors of the understanding, and when Donne turns to errors in the will it becomes clear that, like Hooker, he too held the orthodox theory of theological persecution, for "the edge of the iron should be whetted against such persons". "The law of the prince is rooted in the power of God. The root of all is order, and the orderer of all is the King; And what the good Kings of Judah, and the religious Kings of the Primitive Christian Church did, every King may, nay, should do. For both

[1] His *Pseudo-Martyr*, though the least readable of his works, is quite the most readable pamphlet in the whole of the Oath of Allegiance controversy even if only for the felicities of his style.

[2] *Vide Eighty Sermons*, Sermon 73.

the Tables are committed to him (as well the first that concerns our religious duties to God, as the other that concerns our civil duties to men)."[1] Donne then characterizes as impious, the belief of a Jesuit that the King has nothing to do with matters of religion; for Kings are bound to propagate God's truth.

But it is the defence of sovereignty in *Pseudo-Martyr* wherein Donne most resembles Hooker. *Pseudo-Martyr* is an attempt to prove that Catholics who suffer for refusing the Oath of Allegiance have no claim to martyrdom since they are punished wholly for civil treasons. Like all the apologists of the oath Donne asserts that nothing therein violates the Pope's spiritual jurisdiction,[2] but more particularly than they, he bases his denial of the theory of the indirect temporal power of the Papacy upon the imprescriptible rights of sovereignty. In chapter VI he defines sovereignty as a power infused immediately from God which must exist in any community whatever its form of government. "For those differences which appear to us in the divers forms, are not in the essence of the Sovereignty, which hath no degrees, no additions, nor diminutions, but they are only in those instruments by which this sovereignty is exercised."[3] The aim of all sovereignty is the same—to procure a peaceable and religious life; though Donne thinks that "since the establishing of the

---

[1] *Eighty Sermons*, Sermon 69.

[2] *Pseudo-Martyr*, ed. 1610, chap. XIII.

[3] In chap. XIII, p. 363, Donne does recognize the existence of states where princes are conditional and not absolute sovereigns (as at Venice). Here the power of deposing princes may lawfully be exercised.

Christian Church, God hath testified abundantly, that regal authority, by subordination of bishops is the best and fittest way to those ends".[1] For Donne, therefore, it becomes clear that "if a King be a King upon this condition, that the Pope may, upon such cause as seems just to him, depose him, the King is no more a sovereign than if his people might depose him".[2]

It is, however, important to notice that Donne makes a religious as well as a peaceable life the end of sovereign power. He is not, like Hobbes later, merely allowing the sovereign to use religion for political purposes, though he realizes that the claims of the sovereign to maintain civil peace may lead to the proscription of certain doctrines.[3] As to Hooker,[4] Church and State to Donne are two aspects of one body, and he is theoretically at the other extreme to separatism. "Nor doth the King and Church direct us to divers ends, one to tranquillity, the other to salvation, but both concur in both."[5] "God hath not delivered us over to a Prince only, as to a Physician, and to a Lawyer, to look to our bodies and estates; and to the Priest only, as to a Confessor, to look to and examine our souls, but the Priest must as well endeavour, that we live virtuously and innocently in this life for Society here, as the Prince, by his laws, keeps us in the way to heaven: for thus they accomplish a Regale Sacerdotium where both do both; for we are sheep to them

[1] *Ibid*. chap. VI, p. 168.
[2] *Ibid*. chap. XIII, p. 358.
[3] *Ibid*. chap. V, p. 161.
[4] It is important to notice that *Pseudo-Martyr* appeared in 1610, the eighth book *of Ecclesiastical Polity* not until 1648.
[5] *Pseudo-Martyr*, chap. VI, p. 189.

both, and they in divers relations sheep to one another."[1]

The whole effect of *Pseudo-Martyr*—as with the Canons of 1606—was to replace the divine right of the Pope by the divine right of the King in civil and ecclesiastical affairs—though the power of the King extended not to making new articles of faith but simply to enforcing the truth in God's word. Were the King to do other than this, to enforce, for example, idolatry, Donne would probably have subscribed to the non-resistance doctrines of the abortive canons, but, as with Hooker, it is not a situation that he faces. There can be little doubt that this was the norm of Anglican theory in the early seventeenth century, though concessions were made in practice. The Oath of Allegiance itself was the greatest of these, inasmuch as it admitted that a Roman Catholic might under certain conditions be a loyal Englishman; and Canon 9 of the Canons of 1604,[2] in excommunicating *ipso facto* a Separatist, may, perhaps, be said to have done as much, by implication, for the Separatists.[3] But it is only by implication, and the excommunicate was still under heavy civil disabilities, which made him a poor sort of Englishman. It is true, however, that William Covell, who had written a defence of Hooker, denied, in a conciliatory pamphlet published in 1604, to none the right to live in the State, though he insists on certain disabilities varying in particular cases, according to the type of dissenter. He concludes with a plea for the execution of the penal laws

---

[1] *Pseudo-Martyr*, chap. III, p. 17.   [2] Cardwell, *Synodalia*, I, 249.
[3] Whitley, *Works of John Smyth*, I, p. li.

against Anabaptists, hypocrites, atheists, Jesuits and priests.[1]

Such Anglican replies as were made, therefore, under James to pleas for toleration employ both political and theological arguments. In all cases they were replies to Catholic petitions, as the Catholic problem seemed the more urgent. Gabriel Powel, for example, a polemical divine who spent much of his short life refuting Puritans and Papists, in a pamphlet refuting a Catholic supplication for toleration made in 1603,[2] himself divides his reasons for rejecting the supplication into political and theological. And in certain answers to a supplication of 1604[3] made by both Powel and Matthew Sutclife, Dean of Exeter, a similar combination of arguments is employed. To both, all Papists, with their doctrines of deposition and tyrannicide, are seditious and treacherous, and they show that more advantages are likely to accrue to a state that persecutes Catholics than to a state which tolerates them. Sutclife urges that toleration of Popery is at once dangerous to the State, because of the deposition doctrines; to the King's person, because of the permission to tyrannicide; to the English people because true religion would be in danger; and to all Christians because Papists cause massacres.

[1] Covell, W., *A Modest and reasonable examination of some things now in use in the Church of England, sundrie times heretofore misliked....*

[2] *The Catholics Supplication unto the King's Majesty for toleration of Catholic Religion in England: with short notes or animadversions in the Margin: whereunto is annexed parallelwise a Supplication Counterpoyse of the Protestants...* 1603.

[3] *A Supplication to the Kings Most Excellent Majesty: wherein several reasons of State and Religion are briefly touched...* 1604.

Popery abrogates the sovereignty of the King by denying the Royal Supremacy and by demanding the payment of tribute to a foreign potentate. Where political arguments fail Scripture is invoked. False prophets must be cut down and idolatry destroyed. It is wrong to halt between two opinions, or to tolerate other religion than that of the Apostles. Powel goes so far as to demand the extirpation of idolatry even if it destroys civil peace (it "would be impious to prefer a worldly good to a heavenly one") and urges that though "conscience and religion be not put in by torments", yet persecution may "stirr up a man to consider more seriously the course he holds" —the contention which later largely engaged Locke. Both agree that Puritans are tolerated because they are not seditious, and Sutclife asserts that to refrain from Church is no mere matter of religion but a material act of disobedience to the Prince, and an erroneous conscience "no conscience but mere humour and fancy".[1] In an *Answer to a Catholic Englishman* of 1609 William Barlow likewise makes the Prince the judge of what conscience is permissible in the State. In some sense he tacitly admits the rights of a good conscience (which, of course, Catholic conscience is not) but subjects it to certain limitations—that it must be founded on knowledge and that it must not impugn the authority of the magistrate. For "if pressure of conscience may serve for good plea of recusancy to Prince's laws, there is

[1] Sutclife, M., *The Supplication of Certain Mass-Priests falsely called Catholics....Published with a marginal gloss and answer to the Libellers reasons...* 1604. Powel, G., *A Consideration of the Papists reasons of State and Religion for toleration of popery in England...* 1604.

neither malefactor for crime, nor heretic for schism (never so great) but will make that his apology against any censure. The making of laws and the execution thereof must depend upon the magistrate's will directed by God's word, not upon other men's consciences whether tender as unresolved or peevish as never satisfied".[1] There is, of course, an obvious half-truth in this statement, but what Barlow does not consider is where to draw the line between things that can be left to conscience, and those which necessarily must be under the immediate authority of the magistrate. Like Powel and Sutclife, Barlow further dismisses and justifies Protestant pleas for liberty of conscience at home and abroad (he is apologetic about them) not on the ground of the rights of the Protestant conscience, but for constitutional and political reasons (they are less dangerous, and in some cases subjects have a political right to liberty of conscience).[2] And of course toleration of Catholics is rejected on the general grounds with which we are now familiar that it is against Scripture, dishonourable to the King who has bound himself to maintain the religion he was born in, and dangerous to the State, since clemency breeds plots.

The theory of the power of the Prince in matters of religion was held also by William Laud. In his conference with Fisher the Jesuit, Laud asserted that the Catholic practice of likening the Pope to the sun, and the Emperor to the moon, was "to depress imperial power lower than God hath made it". To the civil power

---

[1] Barlow, W., *Answer to a Catholic Englishman*, p. 51 seq.
[2] *Ibid.* pp. 121-2.

all men, "even to the highest bishop", are subject, "and in spiritual causes too, so the foundation of faith and good manners be not shaken". Emperors and kings are *custodes utriusque tabulae*, and, according to the examples of Hezekiah, Justinian and Charlemagne, they may "proceed to necessary reformations in church business, and therein command the very priests themselves".[1] There is no necessity for one Pope, supreme over the whole Church, to act as infallible judge of controversies, since the King is judge of all temporal differences, and Christ "hath left in his Church, besides his law-book the Scripture, visible magistrates and judges, that is archbishops and bishops under a gracious King, to govern both for Truth and Peace according to the Scripture, and her own canons and constitutions, as also those of the Catholic Church, which cross not the Scripture, and the just laws of the realm".[2]

In matters of doctrine, however, Laud was extremely tolerant, under the influence of the Arminian reaction against the rigid predestinarian doctrines of Calvin. He rejected the doctrine of exclusive salvation. He condemned the Sectaries and Papists for crying that there was no salvation outside their respective churches. It is true that there is no salvation outside the Catholic Church, but neither the Sectarian nor the Roman Church are the Catholic Church by themselves. "Salvation is not shut up into such a narrow conclave."[3]

---

[1] Laud, W., *A relation of the Conference between William Laud . . . and Mr Fisher, the Jesuit*, ed. 1639, p. 205.
[2] *Ibid.* pp. 210–11.　　　　[3] *Ibid.* Preface.

Although, therefore, Fisher denied the possibility of salvation to Protestants, Laud was ready to concede it to Catholics.[1] "The Scripture", moreover, "is sufficient to salvation, and contains in it all things necessary to it."[2] As for doctrinal controversy, though Laud did not regard it as very profitable, he was prepared to admit it, provided it distracted not the peace of the Church. "All consent in all ages, as far as I have observed, to an article or canon, is to itself, as it is laid down in the body of it; and if it bear more sense than one, it is lawful for any man to choose what sense his judgment directs him, so that it be a sense according to the analogy of the faith, and that he hold it peaceably without distracting the Church, and this till the Church which hath made the article determine the sense; and the wisdom of the Church hath been in all ages, or the most, to require consent to articles in general as much as may be, because that is the way of unity, and the Church in high points requiring assent to particulars hath been rent."[3] In a letter from Laud and two other bishops to the Duke of Buckingham in August 1625, defending Montague from the attack upon him in the Commons, Laud urged that at the time of the Elizabethan settlement, the Church of England refused "to be too busy with every particular school point. The cause why she held this moderation was because she could not be able to preserve any unity amongst Christians if men were forced to subscribe to

---

[1] *Ibid.* p. 283.   [2] *Ibid.* p. 52.
[3] Laud's comment on the Resolution on Religion in the Commons of March 1629 wherein the Lower House had taken its stand on the Calvinist interpretation of the Articles. Gardiner, *op. cit.* VII, 124.

curious particulars disputed in schools." As for the opinions maintained by Montague, some are the resolved doctrine of the Church of England: "some of them such as are only fit for schools, and to be left at more liberty for learned men to abound in their own sense, so they keep themselves peaceable and distract not the Church."[1] Here, however, Laud was defending Montague against the intolerance of the Commons. But in a position of power his dislike of dogmatists would cause him to impose silence. The very controversy over Montague's Arminianism ended by Laud imposing silence on his opponents. The Declaration prefixed to the articles of religion, first issued in 1628 and still in the Prayer-Book, commanded all men to submit to the plain literal sense and meaning of the articles, and ordered the repression of those that affixed new meanings to them. The constant, and often reiterated aim of Laud in all his ecclesiastical policy was to join truth with peace. "I have ever with a faithful and single heart (bound to his free grace for it) laboured the meeting, the blessed meeting of Truth and Peace in his Church, and which God, in his own good time will (I hope) effect."[2] "I have moved every stone, that those thorny and perplexed questions might not be discussed in public before the people, lest we should violate charity under the appearance of truth. I have always counselled moderation lest everything should be thrown into confusion by fervid minds to which the care of religion is

---

[1] Laud, *Works* (Library of Anglo-Catholic Theology), VI, part I, 244. Gardiner, *op. cit.* V, 401.
[2] Laud, *Conference with Fisher*, p. 388.

not the first object.... For my own part I will labour with the grace of God that Truth and Peace may kiss one another. If, for our sins, God refuse to grant this, I will hope for eternal peace for myself as soon as possible, leaving to God those who break that kiss asunder, that he may either convert them, as I heartily desire, or may visit them with punishment."[1] Gardiner, commenting on this, says that Laud always put peace before truth, and so order before liberty. As an account of Laud's practice this is true, but in justice to Laud it should be appreciated (and of this Gardiner makes no mention) that he was well aware of the danger of sacrificing the one to the other. "If I can help on to Truth in the Church, and the Peace of the Church together, I shall be glad, be it in any measure. Nor shall I spare to speak necessary Truth, out of too much love of peace. Nor thrust an unnecessary Truth to the breach of that Peace which once broken is not so easily sodered again. And if for necessary Truth's sake only, any man will be offended, nay take, nay snatch at that offence, which is not given, I know no fence for that. 'Tis Truth, and I must tell it."[2]

The means Laud adopted to reconcile Truth and Peace were, however, calculated, as we now see, precisely to frustrate that object. Unity and uniformity he regarded as identical, and he believed thoroughly in the importance of decent order and outward ceremonial because he regarded the outward and visible as the

[1] Laud, *Works*, VI, part I, 263. Letter to J. Vossius. Gardiner, *op. cit.* VII, 124.

[2] Laud, *Conference with Fisher*, Preface.

surest means to the inward and spiritual. "Ever since I came in place, I laboured nothing more than that the external public worship of God (too much slighted in most parts of this kingdom) might be preserved, and that with as much decency, and uniformity as might be; being still of the opinion that unity cannot long continue in the Church, where uniformity is shut out of the door. And I evidently saw that the public neglect of God's service in the outward face of it, and the musty lying of many places dedicated to that service, had almost cast a damp upon the true inward worship of God; which while we live in the body, needs external helps, and all little enough to keep it in any vigour."[1] Laud thus came to require as essential things which, though to him only means to an end, things indifferent, were to the Puritan and Separatist the very marks and badges of anti-Christ. The Puritans suffered more than the Catholics under Laud because they combined in themselves the two things Laud most hated: a fanatical dogmatism disturbing the peace of the Church, and a neglect of the "external worship of God in his Church" which is "the great witness to the world that our heart stands right in the service of God. Take this away, or bring it into contempt, and what light is there left to shine before men, that they may see our devotion, and glorify our Father which is in Heaven?"[2]

The Laudian persecution was thus actuated by motives more theological than moved James in practice.

[1] Laud, *Works*, IV, 60. From the "History of the Troubles and Trials of Archb. Laud". Gardiner, *op. cit.* VII, 127.

[2] Laud, *Conference with Fisher*, Preface.

It is true that there were political reasons for repressing Puritanism. In the letter, which has already been quoted, to the Duke of Buckingham, Laud insists that Parliament should not be allowed to judge Montague, because such a right belongs to the King and bishops in Convocation, and "if the Church is struck down what will follow next?" Had the Puritan Parliament succeeded in the Montague case, it would certainly have been a step further towards political ascendancy. It is true also, that in the *Conference with Fisher* Laud repeatedly denies having persecuted.[1] "God forbid I should ever offer to persuade a persecution in any kind or practise it in the least." But when he continues, it is clear that his denial of persecution is only in name. "But on the other side God forbid too, that your Majesty should let both laws and discipline sleep for fear of the name of persecution", and he urges the defence of the Church against Catholics and Puritans on the ground that it is better to prevent rents in Church or State by wisdom than punish by justice.[2] It is further true that Laud rarely persecuted error as such, and that none suffered for heresy under him, because his conception of truth was a wide one. But he did execute repressive laws and persecute so that God might be worshipped in the way which seemed to him most desirable.

However, it is the theory of the divine right of the Prince in matters of religion, to command for truth, and to reform the Church, and the conception of Church

[1] E.g. p. 375, where Laud denies having taught or forced men to believe one thing and practise another.

[2] Laud, *Conference with Fisher*, Preface.

and State as two aspects of one body, which is of fundamental importance under Charles and Laud, as under James. Strafford, like Lord-Keeper Williams, was no dogmatist and he was not in favour of raising trouble on theoretic and dogmatic grounds,[1] but in a speech at York in 1628 on his appointment by the King to the presidency of the Council of the North, he made some observations to which the Church and the government could well subscribe. "I not only profess my entire filial obedience to the Church, but also covet a sound, a close conjunction with the clergy, the grave the reverend clergy, that they to us, we to them, may as twins administer help to each other; that ecclesiastical and civil institutions, the two sides of every state, may not stand alone by themselves upon their own single wills, subject to cleave and fall in sunder; but joined strongly together in the angle, where his Majesty, under God, is the mistress of the corner, the whole frame may rise up unitate ordinata both in the spirituals and the temporals."[2] It was this conception of what Donne called the "Regale Sacerdotium" against which the Separatist tolerationist had to struggle.

[1] Wedgwood, C. V., *Strafford*, p. 177.
[2] Gardiner, *op. cit.* VII, 29.

CHAPTER IV

THE APPROACH TO THE SEPARATIST IDEA OF RELIGIOUS LIBERTY: THE THEORY OF THE "PURITANS"

IN the two ensuing chapters we shall consider the theory of the Protestant sects in England, and the birth of the separatist idea of religious liberty. It will be seen that as these sects move into a greater degree of separation from the Church of England, their purely theological development is accompanied by a gradual approximation to the separatist idea of religious liberty through the separation of Church and State. From the Presbyterians to the Independents, and from the Independents to the Barrowists there is a logical progression to the theory of the Baptists, in whose thought the idea of religious liberty is first to be found. It would, of course, be erroneous to regard this logical development as chronological also. Ideas never progress in the orderly sequence that events must, but the logic inherent in any one theological position is often a stepping-stone to the next. Nevertheless, this chronological development there is in the theories we are about to consider: that they are almost all developed before 1625, many in the reign of James I himself, and that after the birth of the full separatist idea of religious liberty amongst the Baptists in 1610, the development is both logical and chronological amongst those by whom the idea was accepted. The development of the separatist idea of religious liberty, in other words, takes place in the first part of the period which is at present under consideration, and ceases temporarily with the institution of the Laudian régime.

Further, it should be appreciated that this gradual approximation to the idea of religious liberty is a theoretical and not a practical advance. With the exception of the Baptists, in whose theory the separation of Church and State is absolute, all the sects we shall consider justified the power of the magistrate in religious matters sufficiently to have persecuted as much as each other in practice had they been in a position of power. But their theory of persecution was in each case orientated to a different system of theological and ecclesiastical ideas, and in this their importance lies. For their general theories contained within them the logic which, when carried to extremes, enabled the Baptists to reject the theory of persecution altogether.

I

POLITICAL PURITANISM AND THE PRESBYTERIANS

The term "Puritan" is both ill-defined in itself, and loosely used to cover several religious sects and political parties. In the period before the outbreak of the Civil War it has been applied to the political opposition of the House of Commons to the policy of the Stuarts; to the body of Presbyterian principles which were held by many members of that House, as well as by a minority of the Anglican Church; and to the principles of the Congregational-Independents, who were half separated from that Church. It is, therefore, important to distinguish these component parts of "Puritanism", because although they all were to be united in a common opposition to the policy of King and Church, their theoretical position is by no means identical.

It has been seen how James I frequently pleaded the cause of toleration to a House of Commons more intolerant than he. The justification which the House gave for its attitude was usually more political than theological—the seditious doctrines and practices of the Papists, the intrigues of Spain, and the success of the Counter-Reformation forces abroad[1]—though there is always a tacit assumption that idolatry and the Roman Antichrist can in no wise be tolerated. The House of Commons, as much as the King, saw in religious differences a menace to the safety of the State, but, freed from the responsibility of government, they were inclined to press for a stricter enforcement of the penal laws as a solution for all religious and civil divisions, irrespective of the immediate consequences at home and abroad. (And amongst those whom they would suppress as Papists were some—as Montague—who were accounted friends of the King.) Sir John Eliot, for example, in a speech on 23 June 1625, after suggesting that it is religion which, as a common obligation amongst men, keeps subjects in obedience, urges that

[1] E.g. The Petition of the House of Commons, 3 December 1621. Cobbett, *Parliamentary History*, p. 1323, and the speech of Pym on 28 November. Gardiner, *History of England*, 1603–42, IV, 243.

both the purity and the unity of it must be kept, for where there is division in religion "as it wrongs divinity, so it makes distractions among men, and so dissolves all ties and obligations civil and natural". The religious distractions now in the land can be cured by finding "the cause whence the sickness springs". But it is not in theological intolerance that Eliot finds the cause, as would the historian, wise after the event, for he proceeds to plead for the stricter execution of the penal laws, and for their revision where they prove insufficient.[1] The plea for the stricter execution of the penal laws is a refrain to almost every speech and petition on religion in the House of Commons until Charles began his personal rule. The Commons were, however, actuated as much by fear in their zeal against Papists, as by theological hatred. Sir Robert Phelips in a speech on 26 November 1621 remarks how the Papists have grown insolent—"they call us already the Protestant faction"—and desires "in this respect that we may proceed with some course for our safety at home, that they who are grown to such a head here may not turn the wheel about and so, when they have gotten us under, we mourn and repent our want of consideration and providence".[2] The Petition on religion which proceeded from this debate asserted that the Popish religion "hath a restless spirit and will strive by these gradations; if it once get but a connivance, it will press for a toleration; if that should be obtained they must have an equality; from thence they will aspire to a

---

[1] Eliot, *Negotium Posterorum*, I, 72. Gardiner, *op. cit.* v, 342.
[2] Cobbett, *op. cit.* p. 1306. Gardiner, *op. cit.* IV, 236.

superiority, and will never rest till they get a subversion of the true religion".[1]

Presbyterianism in England during the years 1603 to 1639 produced no theoretical statement of its position comparable with the works of Cartwright and Travers, which must still be taken as representative of their view. Gardiner testifies to a lull in Presbyterian activity during the first and second decades of the seventeenth century,[2] and much of the polemic of these Puritans who desired to remain full members of the Church of England and to change it from within, is concerned merely with proving their position over controverted points and ceremonies from the Scriptures. Many of the more zealous Puritans, after the failure of the Hampton Court Conference, became discontented with mere dissent from the controverted ceremonies whilst remaining full members of the Church, and moved into a greater or less degree of separation from the Church of England. Certainly, theological polemic amongst the more able Puritans comes to concern itself from 1603 to 1625 with the necessity or otherwise of separation from a Church which all of them agreed in regarding as polluted. After 1625, and particularly after the institution of the Laudian régime in 1630, the literature of those Puritans who considered themselves full members of the Church, becomes once more violent and scurrilous as it had been in the days of Martin Marprelate. Under the pressure of the severest persecution it had yet experienced, Puritanism expended its energies on

[1] Cobbett, *op. cit.* p. 1323. Gardiner, *op. cit.* IV, 248.
[2] Gardiner, *op. cit.* III, 238.

attacks on the revival of ceremonial—especially bowing and kneeling—which resulted from Laud's succession to Abbot as Archbishop, and upon scurrilous attacks on the bishops and the institution of prelacy as a whole. Increased persecution had heightened tempers, and it was not likely that such works of the Puritans as escaped the Laudian censorship and saw the light of day would content themselves with reasoned arguments about principles, still less argue toleration. Protest against persecution, of course, there is; but not against persecution in general; merely against persecution of the truth. Henry Burton, for example, in his sermon *For God and King* published in 1636, for which he suffered so heavily, argued, amongst other things, the wickedness of those who persecute ministers merely for maintaining the word of God, but there is no attempt to denounce persecution as such.[1] And, indeed, the Puritan threats to the bishops left no doubt as to what would happen to episcopacy and its supporters were they once to lose their hold of power. The emergence of a doctrinal dispute in the Church over the truth of the Calvinist doctrine of Predestination and the success of the Arminians did, it is true, produce works on matters of general principle, as, for example, in 1626, Prynne's *Perpetuity of a Regenerate Man's Estate.* But these were concerned with matters of pure theology, from which the problem of toleration is less likely to arise than it is from discussions on Church polity and the position of the magistrate in the Church. Moreover, it seems probable that after 1630 it came to be realized that the

[1] Burton, H., *op. cit.* p. 81.

issue between those Puritans who remained members of the Church, and the bishops (as, indeed, the House of Commons suggested it was in respect of Catholics too) was no longer a struggle for toleration but for open supremacy in Church as well as in State.

II

THE CONGREGATIONAL-INDEPENDENTS

It has been seen that the more able Puritan leaders tended, after the Hampton Court Conference, to consider more seriously the question of separation from the Church of England. In some cases this led to important defections to the Separatist congregations abroad, but more usually it led to the adoption of Congregational or Independent principles, which insisted upon nonconformity within the Church of England itself. Burrage has shown that the early Congregationalists were merely a certain type of Puritan, and not full Separatists from the Church of England, although as time went on they approximated more and more to the churches of the Separation.[1] Their opinions, moreover, were not obtained directly from either Brownists or Barrowists, but from Henry Jacob under whose direct influence the early Congregationalists seem to have originated.[2]

In 1604, in the first Congregational catechism ever formulated,[3] Jacob defined "a true visible or ministerial Church of Christ" as "a particular congregation being a spiritual perfect corporation of believers, and having

---

[1] Burrage, C., *Early English Dissenters*, I, 281.
[2] *Ibid.*   [3] *Ibid.* p. 287.

power in itself immediately from Christ to administer all religious means of faith to the members thereof", and asserted that such a church is constituted and gathered "by a free mutual consent of believers joining and covenanting to live as members of a holy society together in all religious and virtuous duties as Christ and his Apostles did institute and practise in the Gospel. By such a free mutual consent also all civil perfect corporations did first begin".[1] Now the idea of the independent, self-sufficient congregation covenanted together by free mutual consent, affected the Anglican conception of the relations between Church and State. How, asks Jacob, shall unity be preserved and obedience to the magistrate, if every particular Church be an entire Church? "Unity in conscience standeth not upon one Church or pastor over the rest, but upon one word and testament of Christ taught ordinarily by that Church unto us whereof we are; as God's ordinance is."[2] So far Jacob favours toleration by refusing to identify unity with mere uniformity. But he finds that his congregational principles are more favourable to the power of the magistrate in the Church than even episcopacy. "Thus most easily may the nearest dwelling magistrate rule any church in outward peace; yea in peace and concord far more easily and readily than otherwise."[3]

The reason why Jacob finds the power of the magistrate in the Church more favoured by congregational principles than by episcopacy is that the former, be-

---

[1] Jacob, H., *Principles and Foundations of the Christian Religion. Vide* C. Burrage, *op. cit.* II, 153.
[2] *Ibid.*   [3] *Ibid.*

lieving in the spiritual self-sufficiency of each congregation, deny any form of jurisdiction to the hierarchy of bishops, and ruling synods, and attribute all coercive power in ecclesiastical affairs directly to the magistrate. In a supplication for toleration of 1605 Jacob proposed certain conditions upon which he thought a toleration might be granted. Puritans would take the Oath of Supremacy and royal authority, keep brotherly communion with the Church of England, and pay all payments and dues ecclesiastical and civil. But further, "if any trespass be committed by any of them whether ecclesiastically or civilly against good order and Christian obedience, then the same person shall be dealt withal therein by any of your Majesty's civil magistrates, and by the same ecclesiastical government only whereunto he ordinarily joineth himself, according as to justice appertaineth, and not to be molested by any other whatsoever".[1] Now the power of censure invested in any congregation (and it is the congregation freely covenanted together, to which Jacob refers when he writes of the "ecclesiastical government to which a man ordinarily joineth himself") had already been defined in the *Principles and Foundations of the Christian Religion*. Church government, it was there stated, should be by elected ministers; and offenders corrected by the whole Church, first admonishing them twice or thrice and exhorting to repentance, and then resorting to excommunication should these fail.[2] That the punish-

[1] Jacob, *A Third Humble Supplication of many faithful subjects in England falsely called Puritans directed to the King's Majesty*, 1605. *Vide* Burrage, *op. cit.* II, 161.
[2] Jacob, *Principles and Foundations. Vide* Burrage, *op. cit.* II, 153.

ment of offenders should proceed no further than these spiritual censures Jacob did not envisage, but he clearly maintained that any further punishment should be at the hands of the civil magistrate. In other words Jacob envisaged a separation of the executors of the two powers, spiritual and temporal, but was not prepared to separate the ends for which they were to be used. He denies coercive power to ruling synods acting over the particular congregation, which is an "entire Church" in itself, but in no wise restricts the power of the magistrate in matter of religion. Thus in *A Christian and modest offer of a most indifferent conference* published in 1606, and written on behalf of "the late silenced and deprived ministers in England", Jacob laid down certain propositions. Amongst these it was declared that "it is simply unlawful for any Pastor under the New Testament to be also a civil magistrate"; "that civil magistrates ought to be overseers of Provinces and Dioceses, and of the several Churches therein. And that it is their office and duty enjoyned them by God to take knowledge of, to punish and redress all misgovernment or ill-teaching of any Church or Church officers." Further it is maintained that such a form of Church government "is more agreeable to the state of a monarchy, and to the King's supremacy in causes ecclesiastical, and more easy and safe both for Church and Commonwealth than is the present government by prelates".[1] This indeed is the often repeated theme of most of Jacob's earlier pamphlets.

Especially, however, is this true of *The Humble*

---

[1] Jacob, *op. cit.* Props. 11, 12, 13.

Supplication for toleration of 1609.[1] The form of toleration therein requested had three main parts. The petitioners pleaded, first, to be allowed to follow God's
ordinances freely in his Church. (Jacob adhered very
literally to Scripture. Though there are indifferent
things in civil matters: "of the parts of divine service
and church use there is nothing at all indifferent. All
such things are here simply commanded or forbidden."[2])
Secondly, they claimed exemption from the prelates and
their officers; and lastly, they pleaded to be allowed to
live under the King and his subordinate magistrates and
to be accountable to them. The first of the three main
reasons advanced in support of this toleration is that
"the Church government solicited is more compatible,
and more advantageous to the King's imperial scepter
than that of the Prelates", a contention which the
petitioners proceed to prove. Whereas the State of
England has all power and jurisdiction within itself
direct from God, and in no way from abroad, both in
Church and Commonwealth, it is clear, they maintain,
that the prelates, in maintaining a ministry by ordination
conveyed to them by Rome, impugn the King's power

---

[1] *To the Right High and Mighty Prince James....An Humble
Supplication for toleration and liberty to enjoy and observe the
ordinances of Christ Jesus in the administration of his churches in lieu
of human institutions.* Reprinted by S. R. Maitland, 1859. Burrage,
op. cit. I, chap. XII, asserts that Jacob was abroad in 1609, and suggests that the *Supplication* may not have been by him. But a later
petition for toleration in 1616 which is certainly by Jacob (*A
Confession and Protestation of the Faith of Certain Christians in
England...*) explicitly refers to the *Supplication* of 1609 as being by
Jacob, or at least by his adherents who shared his views.

[2] Jacob, *Principles and Foundations.*

more than do the petitioners, who teach that all spiritual jurisdiction arises from among themselves. Prelacy is a human institution removable by the King. In holding to the Apostolic succession, however, the prelates deny this point of the Supremacy. The petitioners further hold that all ecclesiastical courts should come from the Crown, and not from the prelates; that civil magistrates should oversee provinces and dioceses, and censure and redress abuses; and that the King may dispose of temporalities (which the prelates deny). Ruling synods of bishops making ecclesiastical laws are unlawful and usurp the powers of the Supremacy, for to the King alone appertains the right of making laws. Nor do the petitioners "partake of the confusion growing from parity (subordination of officers being as natural in the body of Christ as in the body natural)". The only parity that is essential is that between separate congregations, and confusion arises from attempts at subordination.

The second main reason of the petitioners—"reason and policy of State"—is not dissimilar to the first. Toleration, they urge, would pacify contentions by removing the causes of them, and would free the people from the exactions of the bishops, thereby enriching the Crown. It is against the people's wish that episcopacy should be kept, and so against a sound maxim of state. A prince should treat all his subjects equally; for to favour some and censure others produces disaffection. But there is no pretence of this being anything other than an *ex parte* plea for toleration. Not only do they desire the Church to be purged of "Romish reliques" by the magistrate's authority, but they expressly denounce any toleration of Papists as an indulgence to Antichrist, and adduce the argument which, *mutatis mutandis*, had been employed by the Papists, that toleration of themselves will assist in the repression of their common enemy.

The third main reason advanced for toleration is an account of the vexations and rigours of the prelates, but the earlier political reasons are not only more numerous, but more significant in themselves. Jacob adduces no Scriptural, moral, or theological reasons for toleration, nor does he emphasize the wickedness of oppressing conscience. This may, of course, have in part resulted from the petitioners' desire to present those arguments which would most likely be found acceptable to the King. Jacob is more Erastian (in the proper sense of the term) than the bishops themselves. But had Jacob any belief in the rights of conscience and the immorality of persecution they would scarcely have been omitted from this present petition.

From 1609 to 1616 Henry Jacob fled to Holland, where he came under the influence of the Barrowist Churches which had completely separated from the Church of England, and of the numerous Protestant sects which flourished there. In 1616 he returned to London and formed an Independent Puritan Congregation, and published in the same year *A Confession and Protestation of the Faith of Certain Christians in England*.[1] From this it is clear that Jacob's experiences abroad had moved him further towards the position of the

[1] Burrage, *op. cit.* I, 512.

wholly separated Churches, though he never became a Separatist. He is no longer, for example, willing to "tarry for the magistrate",[1] as he had been in 1604,[2] and he considers several questions which can only have been suggested to him by the Churches of the Separation, and over which his views illustrate his midway position between the Anglican Church and the Barrowists. Thus Jacob considers the problem of "scandalous mixtures in the congregation". Now it has been seen that the Barrowists rejected the Anglican Church in part because "all the profane and wicked of the land are received into it", and because they believed that polluted things must be separated from. Jacob, however, held that the admixture of ungodly does not make void the holiness of the assembly, though it does put it into great peril, and a Christian seeking safety might be advised to leave the polluted congregation and join another.[3] The Separatists would have held that ungodly, if not cast out, destroy the value of the assembly as a whole, and that therefore such an assembly should be completely and utterly separated from. In other words Jacob is not prepared to deny the Anglican Church to be a true

---

[1] This is shown by the foundation of his congregation, and from the title of the *Confession and Protestation* of 1616 which goes on to mention "the necessity of observing Christ's ordinances though the same do differ from the common order of the land". *Vide* also *A Collection of Sundry Matters* published in the same year, which emphasizes this point.

[2] *Vide* part of a paper written by Jacob in Burrage, *op. cit.* II, 165, where Jacob denies having exhorted ministers to set up the discipline irrespective of the attitude of the King.

[3] Jacob, *A Confession and Protestation of the Faith of Certain Christians in England.*

Church, though he thinks there are certain things which must be abstained from.[1]

This tendency to approximate to the views of the separated Churches, however, in no way affects Jacob's view of the power of the magistracy in the Church. All true visible Churches "ought to be overseen and kept in good order, and peace, and ought to be governed (under Christ) both supremely and subordinately by the civil magistrate; yea in causes of religion when need is. By which rightful power of his he ought to cherish and prefer the godly and religious, and to punish (as truth and right shall require) the untractable and unreasonable. Howbeit yet always but civilly."[2] This last sentence, taken in conjunction with an ensuing denial of the lawfulness of "committing either spiritual or civil government (viz. diocesan or provincial) to ministers of the word" (for such is a direct transgression of the text of the Gospel), indicates that Jacob still strictly separates the executors of the two powers, spiritual and temporal, though he would allow both to be used by their respective holders for a spiritual end. In the petition for toleration which concludes the *Confession and Protestation* the reasons given are, it is true, less political than before; Jacob urges that "this is the essential order in the Gospel...which we follow", and there is more emphasis on conscience than heretofore. They perceive "that the peril of their souls lieth thereon", and that "to

---

[1] This is further shown by his admission of the validity of Anglican ordination provided that the minister is freely received by his congregation. (*Confession and Protestation.*)

[2] Jacob, *Confession and Protestation.*

deny their faith would violate their conscience". Even so conscience is only slightly treated, and there is no such reliance upon it as Parsons was prepared to put (in part, no doubt, because Jacob, unlike Parsons, had other appeals to rely on).

In the *Third Humble Supplication* Jacob refers with approval to William Bradshaw's *A Protestation of the King's Supremacy*.[1] Bradshaw was one of the first to agree with, and to promulgate the congregational Puritan views of Henry Jacob, and the title of a pamphlet written by him at the same time as the *Protestation of the King's Supremacy*, in which he stated these views with great clearness, suggests that as early as 1605 there was growing up the distinction we have noticed between the Presbyterian Puritan and the Independent, though still non-separatist, type. The pamphlet was entitled *English Puritanism containing the main opinions of the rigidest sort of those that are called Puritans in the realm of England*.[2] In the *Protestation of the King's Supremacy* Bradshaw considered these opinions in relation to the power of the magistrate in the Church, and found, as Jacob, that congregational principles were far more favourable to the Supremacy than episcopacy could ever be. The essence of this pamphlet can be summarized under five headings. It is stated, first, that all jurisdiction and coercive authority in the Church appertains to the King's office, and that the Supremacy must be yielded to it, even if the King in person is an infidel and no member of the Church.[3] Thereby is conceded to the

[1] Published 1605.
[2] Burrage, *op. cit.* I, 287.   [3] Bradshaw, *op. cit.* cap. 4.

86

magistrate the power of making ecclesiastical laws;[1] of removing from the Church anything against the word of God even though the Church should resist;[2] of forcing both lay and ecclesiastical persons to their duties and of punishing ecclesiastical officers for abuses of their authority.[3] Further the King alone may summon synods and authorize canons,[4] and has power to banish from the Church and repress scandalous, schismatic and heretic preachers.[5] Secondly, everything that the King orders in ecclesiastical as well as civil affairs, in so far as it is not against God's word, binds the conscience.[6] The negative form in which this statement is made is important, because it offers a larger field of power to the King than if he had only been conceded power to enforce such things as were directly commanded by God's word, though this is mitigated by the further condition that "the only authority we deny to the King in matters ecclesiastical is such as is proper to Christ. Christ alone is doctor of the Church in matter of religion, and his word is perfect for substance and ceremony."[7] Thirdly, if the King should order anything against God's word, the ministers can but leave him to God, though the power of the Supremacy remains as before.[8] Fourthly, ecclesiastical officers have no coercive jurisdiction whatsoever, but only spiritual power.[9] Their spiritual power, moreover, is only such as is given them by the congregation by whom they are elected, and by whom they

[1] *Ibid.* cap. 8.
[2] *Ibid.* cap. 10.
[3] *Ibid.* caps. 11, 17.
[4] *Ibid.* cap. 14.
[5] *Ibid.* cap. 12.
[6] *Ibid.* cap. 13.
[7] *Ibid.* cap. 22.
[8] *Ibid.* cap. 18.
[9] *Ibid.* cap. 26.

may be deposed,[1] and extends no further than over that congregation.[2] Fifthly, the only power therefore ministers have over the King is the refusal to minister to him, for he is subject to the ecclesiastical censures only of that congregation to which he has expressly joined himself.[3]

It now, therefore, becomes clear why Congregationalists in this period never became theoretical tolerationists. It is true that their theory of the nature of the visible Church subverted the Anglican conception of Church and State as two aspects of one body. It is true also that the idea of a democratic Church formed by a free covenant was, in other circumstances, to lead more directly to the idea of toleration; but the essential part of that theory, which destroys the primary error of theological persecution (that men can be forced into salvation), was never held by either Jacob or Bradshaw. Both believed that the Anglican Church containing "all the ungodly of the land" was in essence a true Church; and they were not therefore prepared to confine the true Church to a freely convenanted body of regenerated persons, to whose regeneration the civil power of the magistrate could in no wise assist. It is further true that Jacob and Bradshaw advocated the strict separation of the executors of the spiritual and temporal powers. But they made no real attempt completely to separate the ends for which these powers are to be used. For any full theory of toleration which is to come by way of the

---

[1] Bradshaw, *English Puritanism.*
[2] Bradshaw, *Protestation,* cap. 24.
[3] *Ibid.* cap. 16.

separation of Church and State, it is essential that both these separations, of powers and of ends, should be fully stated and appreciated. It is no use denying coercive power to the Church if it is to be let out again to the magistrate. It can only become effective (from the point of view of toleration) by separating the end of the State from that of the Church, and by realizing that although spiritual means may be used to further a temporal end, it is never permissible to use civil force for a spiritual end. In other words there is no full statement of the Separatist conception of toleration until the point which Locke so emphasized is appreciated, i.e. "that the Commonwealth is a society of men constituted only for the procuring, preserving and advancing their own civil interests".[1] The confusion and persecution which has arisen as the result of identifying the ends of Church and State are as grave as those arising from the permission granted to either to use indiscriminately both powers. The mediaeval Catholic Church realized and practised in some degree a separation of the temporal sword from the spiritual sword, but persecution existed because both might be used for the same spiritual end. It is therefore as essential a step towards the idea of toleration to separate the ends of Church and State as to realize that different powers must be in different hands.

John Robinson, the pastor of the Pilgrim Fathers, was, however, prepared to take more steps in this direction than either Jacob or Bradshaw. Robinson was a man of some culture and of considerable breadth of mind, and his closer approximation to the separatist idea of tolera-

[1] Locke, *A Letter concerning Toleration.*

tion is due to the fact that at one time he regarded himself as completely separated from the Church of England. This was in 1610, when he removed himself and about a hundred of his company from Scrooby to Leyden. There, however, he held conferences on the subject of separation with Jacob and Dr Ames, another Independent Puritan, with the result that by 1618 he laid aside his more rigid separatist views for those of the non-separatist Independent Puritans.[1]

In 1610 Robinson published a justification of his then separatist position entitled *A Justification of Separation from the Church of England, against Mr Richard Bernard, his invective entitled The Separatists Schism.* Robinson's views on the magistracy, the relationship between Church and State and the two powers, are only incidentally, and not systematically, expressed in this work, but they may be summarized as follows. First, he insists upon the separation of the executors of the two powers, and in part of the ends for which they are to be used. Matters civil "do come under the general administration and government of the world, and do represent the outward man for his present life. On the other side matters ecclesiastical come under the special administration of the Church and serve for the edification and building up of the inward man to eternal life". In civil matters therefore magistrates may command in their own names, and must always be obeyed even if they hurt the subject. "But in causes ecclesiastical not so. There is no King of the Church but Christ...no lord but Jesus....And all his laws and statutes tend to the

[1] Burrage, *op. cit.* I, 293.

furtherance and advancement of every one of his subjects in their spiritual estate, and neither King nor Caesar may nor ought to impose any law to the least prejudice of the same, neither are they therein if they should to be obeyed." In civil matters therefore we obey for the authority of the commander. In ecclesiastical matters we obey the magistrate "only for the ends of the things commanded and as they tend to the edification of ourselves and others".[1] Now there is nothing in this definition with which Jacob could not have agreed, but, as will appear, Robinson excludes from things "tending to edification" certain actions which Jacob would have regarded as permissible and included. Secondly, it follows that as it is wrong to give any civil power whatsoever to ecclesiastics,[2] so the power of the magistrate in the Church to enforce such things as tend to edification, is a power purely civil. "The King indeed is to govern in causes ecclesiastical but civilly, not ecclesiastically, using the civil sword, not the spiritual for the punishing of offenders." To make the King a Church officer would imply that he should be called to his office and deposed from it by the Church,[3] and would deny him the use of his civil power in ecclesiastical causes, since Church officers may employ spiritual means only. Thirdly, Robinson gives a preciser definition of these powers of the magistrate in causes ecclesiastical, and explains what he considers as "tending to

---

[1] Robinson, J., *op. cit.* chap. I, sect. III, p. 31 (of collected works, vol. II).

[2] *Ibid.* chap. III, Error 6, p. 174.

[3] *Ibid.* p. 278, Error 8.

edification". The magistrate may use his civil power to prevent a true Church from becoming corrupt, i.e. he may suppress idolatry and see that no wicked person is taken into or kept in the Church; as also he may provide "that the truth of God in his ordinance be taught and published in his dominions; and it may be not unlawful for him, by some penalty or other to provoke his subjects universally into hearing for their instruction and conversion; yea to grant he may inflict the same upon them, if after due teaching they offer not themselves unto the Church".[1] Further, the magistrate is the preserver of both tables of the law, and may "punish all breaches of both, especially such as draw with them the violation of positive laws of kingdoms, or disturbance of common peace".[2] But in no wise may the magistrate command anything against the word of God. More especially no king, "either of Judah or of England, had or hath power from God, to compel an apparent profane person, so remaining, either to join unto, or continue in the Church, and the Church so to receive and continue him". Nor may the King follow the example of the Kings of Judah and destroy all the wicked in the land, since he has not, as had the Kings of Judah, "to gather a national Church".[3]

It is in these last two points that Robinson the Separatist is distinguished from Jacob, and they result from the separatist belief that a true visible Church must consist of the regenerate only. Now regeneration is the gift of God, and therefore the magistrate may not

[1] Robinson, J., *op. cit.* p. 315, i.e. for preparation for conversion.
[2] *Ibid.* p. 193.   [3] *Ibid.* p. 315.

force men into the Church, for to do so would be to invalidate the Church into which they were forced. The Anglican Church is no true Church in part because its constitution under Elizabeth was not voluntary, i.e. it was constituted, not by a free covenant, but by the sole authority of the magistrate, who included within it all the ungodly in the land.[1] Jacob, of course, had insisted on a free covenant, but he would not go so far as to deny the validity of the Anglican Church because it lacked a free covenant, or could only be said to have one by specious argument, and therefore he insisted less upon the necessity for regeneration as a *sine qua non* of a true Church. But it is precisely the separatist belief that a true Church is no longer, as it was under the Kings of Judah, a national Church containing the whole land within it, but a freely covenanted body of the godly, that destroys the primary error of theological persecution— that men can be forced into salvation. The power there- fore that Robinson as a Separatist conceded to the magistrate was largely negative—to protect the true Church from corruption—and positive only in so far as men might be forced to hear the word, and be punished for refusing the instruction necessary to a free con- version.

In his later works, when he had moved into the Independent position, Robinson never insists upon the absolute necessity of freely covenanted Churches of the godly, and his views become more closely those of Jacob. This process of transition is visible in a work published in 1614 in reply to the Baptists, whose separatism, as will

[1] *Ibid.* pp. 318 *seq.*

93

be seen later, was even more extreme than that of the Barrowists.[1] There he argued that those separated from the national Church may communicate in private prayer, etc. with the godly of that Church who still remain members of it through infirmity. He also expressly repudiated the Baptist view of the magistrate's authority in the Church, which implied full religious toleration through the complete separation of Church and State. In reply to the Baptist argument that Christ's disciples should love their enemies, and not kill them or persecute them, Robinson says that the godly magistrate may do both, just as God punishes with temporary death those He loves; and to the further argument that the magistrate ought not to meddle with religion or matters of conscience because Christ is King and lawgiver of the Church and conscience, Robinson replies that this merely proves that though the magistrate may not command against Christ, he yet may lawfully use his lawful power for the furtherance of Christ's kingdom and laws. In support of this contention he quotes the Book of Revelation as saying that kings shall make the whore desolate, and shall use their civil power at first for the beast, but then against it. Moreover kings are nursing fathers of the Church. In 1618, in certain articles sent by the Church of Leyden to the Council of England explaining the position of the Pilgrim Fathers, Robinson compromised even further. Whereas previously he had utterly denied civil power to ecclesiastics,[2] and agreed with Jacob that the belief in

[1] Robinson, *Of Religious Communion Private and Public.*
[2] *In Justification of Separation*, pp. 172 seq.

episcopacy as *jure divino* derogated from the Supremacy,[1] he is now prepared to acknowledge bishops in so far as their authority as overseers over dioceses is derived entirely from the civil magistrate, and that they proceed civilly only, according to the law of the land, and are responsible to the King. No Synod, he therefore maintains, may have power save from the King.[2] This is a neat compromise, because it combines the recognition of bishops with the strict separation of the executors of the civil and ecclesiastical powers, by making bishops in their ruling capacity virtually civil magistrates. In 1619 and 1623, at first in Latin, then in English, Robinson published *A Just and Necessary Apology of Certain Christians...called Brownists or Barrowists*. The term "Brownist" or "Barrowist", as Robinson's title implies, was loosely used as a term of reproach to any who were in a position of greater or less separation, and the work is actually a justification of the views of his Church at Leyden. The views on the magistrate here expressed are precisely those of Jacob, though there is much emphasis on a point which Jacob had held but not unduly emphasized—that the power of the magistrate in religious affairs is attached to his office and not to his person. The power of the magistrate is the same, be he Christian or heathen. Christianity only sanctifies and does not add to the magistrate's power. The Prince rules as Prince, and subjects obey as subjects, not as "faithful" since only Christ has the faithful as subjects. If a Christian magistrate had more power

[1] *Ibid*. p. 39.
[2] S.P. Colonial, I, 43. Gardiner, *op. cit.* IV, 170.

95

than a heathen it would follow that an idolatrous magistrate should have less—which would be seditious. All magistrates therefore have power as God's ministers for the good of their subjects to procure by lawful means whatever appertans "to their natural or spiritual life, so the same be not contrary to God's word".[1] In some sense this position is more Erastian than the pure godly prince theory because it allows the magistrate power in religious affairs simply as magistrate, irrespective of whether he is godly. In another sense it is less, because it denies the magistrate to be an officer of the Church. In other hands, however, which were not prepared to concede any power to the magistrate in matter of religion, the argument that the power of the magistrate is the same be he Christian or heathen, becomes one of the great logical supports of the full separatist idea of toleration.

Towards the end of his life Robinson published a series of *Essays or Observations, Divine and Moral*. These essays, though they are more theological than those of Bacon, have an almost Baconian wisdom and pithiness of style which pierces to the very heart of the subject in the opening sentence of the essay. In the essay "Of Religion, and the differences and disputations thereabout" Robinson considers explicitly the problem of toleration, and though the views there expressed are consistent with his opinions on the magistracy, he now makes an almost latitudinarian approach to the question. Castellion would have agreed that "disputations in religion are sometimes necessary, but always dangerous"

[1] Robinson, *A Just and Necessary Apology*, chap. XI.

because they "draw the best spirits into the head from the heart". Acontius would have approved of his account and explanation of the fickleness of human opinion, and there is an objectivity in his observations which is lacking in most theological polemic, and which no fanatic could ever have achieved. "The most count it the best and safest way in differences of religion without further question to take the strongest part, that doing as the most do, they may have the fewest find fault with them. Such forget God who is strongest of all." Men plead for toleration according as to whether their party is in power or not. "Where the world goes on their side" few of those who have previously cried toleration are themselves prepared to tolerate (just as the early Church began to persecute when it had the Emperor on its side). But considering "that to tolerate is not to approve"; that "magistrates are lords over men properly, and directly as they are their subjects, and not as they are Christ's" and that by accident subjects of the magistrate are also subjects of Christ; and seeing that God is not pleased with unwilling worship, the saying of the wise King of Poland is approvable—that the acceptance of a religion through the heart is one of the three things God has kept in His own hand. Three objections against this are considered and refuted. First, the order in Israel is no example, because Israel was a separated nation in a holy land with its kings, types and figures of Christ—which no land now is. Secondly, it is true that men may be constrained by the magistrate to outward acts of justice though they be destitute of inward virtue; but these serve for the preservation of civil societies, and therefore though they be done unwillingly they achieve their end. Religious actions, however, are not concerned with civil society properly, nor are they attainable but by faith and devotion in the heart. Thirdly, in reply to St Augustine's argument that many who first serve God by compulsion learn afterwards to serve Him freely, it is urged that unreasonable violence produces hypocrites, and that to force a man to practise against his conscience, may constrain him to lose all conscience. Robinson does not, however, deny all compulsion in matter of religion. He does not allow civil disobedience palliated with religious shows, and he permits compulsion for the restraint of public idolatry, and to force man to the hearing of God's word so that religion may be allowed to work. But the magistrate should remember that even in the most anti-Christian sect there may be some few led by the spirit of Christ (*mutatis mutandis*, this is exactly the second reason by which John Stuart Mill defends liberty—that even in the worst error there may be some grain of truth).[1] Further, as the power of the magistrate is from God, which his Christianity, if indeed he be Christian, sanctifies and directs; and as he therefore should use it for God's honour and worship and against the contrary, yet there are always two cautions. First, idolatry and heresy (however great sins in themselves) do not so outlaw a subject civilly as do, for example, seditions and murders which directly violate civil society. Secondly, no human authority may bring into or uphold in the Church, any doctrine or ordinance of religion, or person, unto which God's word

[1] Mill, J. S., *On Liberty*, chap. II.

98

does not give approbation, seeing that magistrates are "no governors against, nor besides, but under God, in their dominions".

It is clear, therefore, that although Robinson's views on the magistrate are those of the Independents, he remains an extreme Independent. The essay examined above is undoubtedly the nearest approach to the full idea of religious toleration which we have yet examined. In part this is the result of Robinson's experiences when he completely separated himself from the Church of England, but it is also due to the breadth and objectivity of his mind. His is the nearest approach that has yet been made to the complete separation of Church and State. In the same essay "Of Religion" he asserts "that the bond between magistrate and subject is entirely civil, but religious accidentally only, though eminently". Because he believed in an absolute truth, known and ascertained, which it was righteous to defend by force against error, and because he believed that men may rightly be forced to have the seed of faith sown in their hearts, even if their conversion must be free, Robinson never arrived at the idea of religious liberty. For that can only come when it is appreciated that in questions of truth and error, force, by its nature, is entirely *extra litem*.

Dr Ames, who with Jacob assisted to bring Robinson to Independency, spent most of his life abroad, but he remained in the Independent position of half-separation, and shared their views on the magistracy. A withdrawal from the true Church is necessary in some cases, where, for example, continued communion would

99   7-2

mean communion in sin, or where there is danger of being seduced into error. But any separation so made might only be a partial separation, so far as to withdraw from sin.[1] The chief care of the magistrate is to promote true religion and repress impiety,[2] and in *A Fresh Suit against Human Ceremonies* Ames envisaged this power as extending to a duty to bring the Church of England out of the corruptions of Rome, and to rid her of all traces of her former estate.[3] But the Church of England, brought forth or not from the traces of her former estate, Ames always regarded as in essence a true Church —a position which the full Separatist was not prepared to accept.

[1] Ames, W., *De Conscientia et ejus jure vel casibus*, 1630, Bk. v, chap. XII.

[2] *Ibid.* chap. XXV.

[3] Ames. *op. cit.* Preface.

CHAPTER V

THE BIRTH OF THE SEPARATIST IDEA OF RELIGIOUS LIBERTY: THE THEORY OF THE SEPARATED CHURCHES

I

THE BARROWISTS

AFTER the execution of Barrow, Greenwood and Penry, the Barrowists in England emigrated to Holland, where, in the period at present under consideration, they lived under the spiritual leadership of Francis Johnson, Henry Ainsworth, and later John Canne.[1] It has been seen that under Elizabeth, the Barrowists approximated more nearly to the separatist idea of toleration than any other sect. During the years 1603–39 there is no change in their theoretical position which brings them closer to the idea of toleration. But, as Robinson's position when he was in complete separation has perhaps suggested, the Barrowist conception of the functions of the magistrate in the Church is more advanced towards the idea of toleration than is the theory of an Independent Puritan like Jacob. And in the minds of the Baptists, some of the positions which the Barrowists had first advocated in England were to lead to the complete separatist idea of toleration implying religious liberty.

[1] Burrage, C., *Early English Dissenters*, I, chap. VI.

The difference, however, between the conception of the magistrate's office held by the Independent Puritan, and of that held by the Barrowist was slight and of emphasis rather than matter. Both Independents and Barrowists regarded the Church of England as polluted and imperfect, and they were agreed upon the nature of these pollutions and imperfections. John Canne, in *A Necessity of Separation from the Church of England* published in 1634—the fullest and clearest statement of Barrowist principles formulated during this period— cites seventy errors of the Church of England condemned by the Independents themselves, with which condemnation the separated Churches of the Barrowists were in the fullest agreement. The Barrowists and Independents were not, of course, agreed in their conclusions as to the course of action which these pollutions and imperfections warranted. The former argued the necessity of complete separation, the latter nonconformity within the Church of England itself. But again the difference is in some sense in degree and emphasis rather than in matter, so much so that Canne, in the aforementioned work, proved the necessity of separation from the Church of England, not from the published principles of the Barrowists, but by the principles of the nonconformists themselves, with which they were largely identical.

Now the difference in the degree of separation required by the Barrowist and Independent sprang, as has been seen in the case of Robinson, from the importance the Barrowist attached to the visible Church as consisting only of truly regenerate and godly persons. We have seen Jacob's compromise on this point, and his view was shared by other Independents, especially by Ames. But to the Barrowist it would not suffice merely to separate from unlawful things so far forth as to separate from sin, still acknowledging the Church which contained them to be in essence a true Church, for "scandalous admixtures" of godly and ungodly in the congregation for him destroyed the lawfulness of the Church as a whole. "What manner of people are there joined together in your Church?" writes Henry Ainsworth in 1608, in reply to a Puritan minister in Gloucester. "Are not there all sorts of profane, wicked, and irreligious persons, as well as religious men of better life....Neither are your people saints by calling; nor can you say of your Church of England that all the building (of all the parishes) coupled together groweth to one holy temple in the Lord; for yourself here defend not all but the best only. And we know well, that the multitudes of profane wicked persons and miscreants, mere strangers and foreigners are of the matter of your Church."[1] Out of the Church, therefore, are to be cast not only "all such as sin against the law of God by error or corruption, in doctrine or conversation", but out of the Church, also, are to be kept "all such as are profane, worldly and wicked until they be called of God unto repentance and faith in his promise".[2]

[1] Ainsworth, H., *Counterpoison. Considerations touching the points in difference between the godly ministers and people of the Church of England and the seduced brethren of the Separation...examined and answered*, 1608, p. 60.
[2] *Ibid.* pp. 122–3. "Positions concerning a True Church."

A freely covenanted body, therefore, of truly regenerate persons is, for the Barrowist, a *sine qua non* of a true visible Church. The Church of England is not the true body of Christ, because it was first instituted from the body of Antichrist (the Papists of Queen Mary's days) "who all (except some few that of themselves refused) were, at the beginning of Queen Elizabeth's reign, received into the body of the Church, and so have continued. . . . Yet they did not then enter in by repentance and faith in Christ (which two things are the beginning and the foundation of the kingdom of God) but by the commandment of the magistrate were compelled into the Church, sacraments, ministry, which then were by law established and ever since continued. Now the magistrate's law cannot work faith in any; seeing faith is the gift of God and his word only is wrought in men's hearts. So that the magistrate though he ought to abolish idolatry, and set up God's true worship, to suppress all errors and cause the truth to be taught; yet cannot he constrain men to join unto the Church, but they must do it willingly and gladly the Lord persuading them thereunto. And these (of whom we speak) not being persuaded by the Lord and his word, but (as the worldly multitude always is) being ready to receive any religion that the Prince would establish, rather than they would suffer persecution, were, in that their popish estate the body of anti-Christ yet then compelled and united unto this Church. Again not only those that were popishly devout and superstitious; but such also as were profane and irreligious, atheist, blasphemous, whoremongers, thieves, drunkards and all other ungodly persons were received and remain in that Church."[1]

The power of the magistrate, therefore, in ecclesiastical affairs does not extend to forcing men to be members of churches, but only to defending true religion when once it has been established by a free covenant. The reformation carried out by Queen Elizabeth is no parallel to the reformations of the Kings of Judah, because Judah was a true Church whereas Elizabeth found a false Church. "Abijah, the predecessor of Asa, maintained God's true religion and worship against idolatrous Israel both by word and sword. So Asa found not his kingdom a false Church as King Edward and Queen Elizabeth found England."[2] Though Judah fell into sin she remained a true Church "and was not (as Israel) quite broken off". "And therefore the magistrate compelled not the people to be members, but to perform the duties thereof, they being truly members before." If Josiah had forced the Edomites, and Egyptians "into the holy temple, and there to have sacrificed to the Lord, it would have been something like unto" Elizabeth's practice. "For the English nation consisting of many shires, cities, towns, villages was never within the Lord's covenant...as Judah was. Howbeit, it may be many hundred years past there were some true Churches planted in the land, by the preaching of the Gospel and obedience of faith."[3] Hezekiah and

---

[1] Ainsworth, H., *op. cit.* p. 127: "Arguments disproving the present estate and constitution of the Church of England."

[2] *Ibid.* p. 229.

[3] Canne, J., *A Necessity of Separation*, p. 223 (Hanserd Knollys Society ed.).

Josiah defended true religion from idolatry by the sword. "These examples we acknowledge all Christian Princes should follow; having equal power with these Kings of Judah to abolish all idolatry within their dominions, yea and to punish obstinate idolaters, and not suffer any superstitious worship amongst their subjects; but to procure their conversion by the word, yet not to compel them to be members of the Church, because they cannot give them faith and repentance, which is the only door into Christ's kingdom, and cannot be opened unto any but by God alone."[1] "Howsoever parents and masters are to use all good means that those which are under their government are religious and holy, yet have they not any power to make them members of God's Church (if they be not under the visible covenant) than they have power to give them saving grace and sanctification."[2] "Such compulsion unto religion persuadeth not the heart, maketh men hypocrites not true Christians, which not only God's word but even the light of reason teacheth."[3] For there is no precedent for forcing men to be members of churches "unless it be taken from Mahomet's doctrine, who taught that men should be compelled to faith by war and sword".[4]

The advance of the Barrowist from the position of the Independent Puritan towards the separatist idea of toleration is thus exactly the advance which Robinson made on Jacob in the days of his complete separation.

---

[1] Ainsworth, *op. cit.* p. 230.   [2] Canne, *op. cit.* p. 222.
[3] Ainsworth, *op. cit.* p. 134.
[4] Canne, *op. cit.* p. 225.

As with the Independent, the Barrowist conception of the visible Church as a freely covenanted congregation having all spiritual power within itself, subverted the Anglican conception of Church and State as two aspects of one body. Like the Independent also the Barrowist insisted upon the strict separation of the two powers, spiritual and temporal. Indeed, his insistence was the stricter, and Canne expressly repudiated the compromise Robinson had made over bishops, which Bradshaw defended. More emphatically, however, than the Independent the Barrowist insisted also upon a partial separation of the ends for which these powers were to be used. He conceded power to the magistrate only to defend true religion, and asserted his utter incapacity to establish a true Church, or to force men to become members of it when established—thereby, as we have seen, destroying the primary error of theological persecution—that men can be forced into salvation. Moreover, as the Barrowist denied to the civil authority power to interfere in certain religious actions, so he was also careful that the spiritual power of excommunication which he gave to each congregation should not interfere with the civil rights of the State or of its citizens. Canne insists that although the faithful must have "no familiar conversation" with an excommunicated impenitent sinner, that they must "cut him civilly in eating, drinking, buying and selling; yet only so far as they are not bound unto him by any of the bonds of civil right and society". Family relationships must remain; all lawful contracts be performed, and "an excommunicate magistrate remaineth a magistrate still, and must of all

Christians be so acknowledged".[1] It is, however, true that this difference between the Barrowist and the Independent is of degree rather than matter. The Independent, as we have seen, did insist upon a free covenant, and some measure of separation from imperfections and pollutions. But it is precisely the greater degree of emphasis that the Barrowist lays upon the Church of freely covenanted "saints" as the only true visible Church, which brings him closer to the full separatist idea of toleration.

The Barrowist position remains nevertheless a theoretical rather than a practical contribution. In practice their theory meant little more than that the Separatists should be free to form churches of their own, and that none might be admitted to them but such as they desired. And had the Barrowists been in power, although none would have been compelled into the Church, with the exception of the Puritans all religious sects in seventeenth-century England would have been persecuted on one or other of the grounds which have been enumerated; and even the Puritans would have been forced to hear the Barrowist interpretation of God's word. In other words although they would have denied that men can be forced into salvation, they would still have persecuted error as such because it is offensive to God and dangerous to man. But even so Barrowist theory is of considerable importance, because it was from the Barrowist position that certain Separatists were to adopt the principles of the Baptists, and with them the idea of religious liberty.

[1] Canne, *op. cit.* p. 146.

THE ARMINIAN BAPTISTS

In 1603 there were no English Baptists. The history of
their origin is largely an account of the spiritual progress
of John Smyth, sometime fellow of Christ's, from
Anglicanism to the principles held by the Waterland
Mennonite congregation which we have seen was
settled at Amsterdam. In the *Justification of Separation*
Robinson testified to Smyth's spiritual instability,[1]
which is "his sin and our cross"; but, although Smyth
suffered periods of great spiritual uncertainty,[2] his progress from Anglicanism to Baptism was in some sense a
carrying to their logical conclusion of the principles
which were inherent in any degree of separation. From
1600, when he was lecturer to the city of Lincoln, he
gradually moved to the position of the Independent
Puritan; thence, with the foundation of his freely
covenanted congregation at Gainsborough, to the position of the Barrowists; and so to the principles of the
Baptists (as they were to be called) who carried separatist principles to their logical conclusion by rejecting
even the baptism of the Anglican Church, and insisting
upon the baptism of truly regenerate adults as an
essential condition of admittance to the true visible
Church.

During the course of this spiritual progress Smyth's
views on the magistracy move in accordance with the

[1] Robinson, *op. cit.* p. 62.
[2] *Vide* Burgess, H. W., *Smyth the se-Baptist Helwys and Baptist
origins*, pp. 69–74.

state of his theological beliefs. *A Pattern of True Prayer*, published in 1605, but preached much earlier, represents Smyth as a full conformist, expounding, with an almost fierce intolerance, the theory of the godly prince, and explicitly condemning toleration as a state in which God's kingdom is shouldered out of doors by the kingdom of the devil.[1] In *Principles and Inferences concerning the visible Church* of 1607, when Smyth was wavering between Independency and Barrowism, his view of the magistracy represents a compromise between these two, though inclining the more to Independency. Princes may still erect churches and "command all their subjects to enter into them, being first prepared and fitted thereto"—implying, as other parts of the work suggest, that they must first be regenerate saints. But on the other hand if the Prince will not reform the Church it must be separated from, not tarrying for the magistrate, until such time as it is reformed.[2] *Parallels, Censures and Observations*, published in 1609, when Smyth had been a year in Amsterdam as a Barrowist, contains an almost similar, though more detailed analysis of the magistrate's power, but his views on this matter seem less advanced than those of Ainsworth at the same

[1] Smyth, *Works*, ed. Whitley, I, 160 *seq*. Whitley suggests that Smyth's fierce intolerance here may have been expressed, as a result of the Gunpowder Plot, after the main body of the work had been composed. Whitley also points out that strictly speaking Smyth never confirmed or denied Independency, and that as a Barrowist he differed from Ainsworth in the democratic powers he conceded to the congregation. "Independent" and "Barrowist" applied to Smyth are, however, convenient terms to indicate his approximate theological position.

[2] *Ibid*. pp. 258 *seq*., especially pp. 263, 267.

period. Though the magistrate may only command "all men to walk in the ways of God if they are fitted and prepared thereto" (he does not explicitly say, as before, that he may force them to be members of churches), there is no emphasis on permission to the magistrate to defend only true religion, nor any explicit denial of his power to erect true churches.[1] This work was actually published after Smyth had baptized himself and then his congregation, but it represents Smyth the Barrowist, and was written long before he contemplated the adoption of believer's baptism. In *The Character of the Beast*, however, published later in the same year, in which Smyth defended his adoption of believer's baptism, he expressed great indecision as to the power of the magistrate. There must, of course, be submission to them for conscience' sake as "the ministers of God for our wealth"; but "of magistrates converted to the faith and admitted into the Church by baptism, there may many questions be made which to answer neither will we if we could, neither can we if we would".[2] It was thus the adoption of the principles of the Anabaptists which reorientated Smyth's mind to the problem of persecution. The early Anabaptists[3] and the Mennonites[4] in Amsterdam had both insisted on the entirely spiritual nature of Christ's kingdom, and therefore of the powers of His Church, and had only permitted

---

[1] *Ibid.* p. 518. [2] *Ibid.* p. 572.

[3] *Vide* Anabaptist Articles printed for Swabians and Swiss in 1527 (especially Article 6) in McGlothlin, *Baptist Confessions of Faith.*

[4] *Vide* Waterland Mennonite Confession of 1580 (especially Article 37) in McGlothlin, *op. cit.*

the magistracy to use the sword to punish evil in the world, not in the Church. And since magistracy involved "war, depriving enemies of goods or life... which do not agree with the lives of Christians who ought to be dead to the world", Anabaptists "withdrew themselves from such offices and administrations".[1] The whole Anabaptist tradition was one of complete reliance upon the New Testament only, making the Old Testament wholly "figurative", and upon the spirituality of Christ's kingdom under the new covenant, replacing the carnal covenant of the Old Testament. So long as Smyth held the Independent Separatist view that although the ministers of God may not use civil force in religious matters, yet in certain ways may the magistrate do so, it was impossible for him to become a complete tolerationist. The objection of the Independent and of the Barrowist was not to the use of civil force in religious matters but to the use of it by a minister of the Church. The Anabaptist attitude was to assert that force, by whomsoever employed, was wholly incompatible with the assumption and practice of a religious faith, and therefore that in no wise could religious matters be the concern of the civil magistrate.

When, however, Smyth published the first Baptist Confession of twenty articles towards the end of 1609, his views on the magistracy were still insufficiently resolved for him to include an article on that subject.[2] In 1610, in the course of negotiations for union with the Mennonites, he subscribed, with most of his con-

[1] Mennonite Confession of 1580. Article 37.
[2] Smyth, *Works*, II, 682.

gregation, to a Confession of thirty-eight articles drawn up by the Mennonites, and almost identical with their Confession of 1580. An article on the magistracy was included, but although Smyth subscribed to it, it is more representative of the views of the Mennonites than of Smyth, because the whole problem of the lawfulness of the magistracy was the real impediment to the union of Smyth's congregation with the Mennonites, and many of Smyth's congregation found themselves unwilling to condemn magistracy as absolutely unlawful to a Christian. Magistracy, the article stated, is a necessary ordinance of God to preserve the civil estate, and the commands of the magistrate must be obeyed "in all causes not contrary to the word of the Lord". The meaning of the phrase "not contrary to the word of the Lord" is enormously extended in the mind of an Anabaptist. In the works, for example, of Robinson, this phrase would allow the magistrate power in religious causes, but in the view of the Anabaptists any use of force in religious matters was contrary to the word of the Lord. The article then proceeds explicitly to deny that a Christian may hold the magistrate's office.[1] In 1610, however, Smyth issued a Confession of a hundred articles on his own account, embodying, two years before his death, the final result of his long spiritual progress.[2] In four articles he stated his views on the magistracy. Christ has commanded all men to be

---

[1] Burrage, *op. cit.* II, 187 *seq.*, Article 35.
[2] Smyth, *Works*, II: "Propositions and Conclusions concerning the true Christian Religion containing a Confession of the Faith of certain English people living at Amsterdam."

subject to the higher powers for conscience' sake. Magistracy is therefore "a permissive ordinance of God" to preserve justice and civility amongst men for the good of mankind. A magistrate may thus "please God in his calling in doing that which is righteous and just". The magistrate, however, "is not by virtue of his office to meddle with religion or matters of conscience", or to force men to any form of religion; but he must "leave Christian religion free to every man's conscience, and handle only civil transgressions, injuries and wrongs" for "Christ only is the King and lawgiver of Church and conscience". If the magistrate would follow Christ he must deny himself and take up his cross. He must love his enemies, not kill them or persecute them, and he himself must suffer persecution for Christ's sake "and that by the authority of magistrates, which things he cannot possibly do and retain the revenge of the sword".[1]

With the exception of *Utopia* this is the first full statement of religious toleration, implying religious liberty, in the English language. It differs from the Mennonite articles Smyth subscribed to in the following ways. First, it emphasizes more the value of the magistrate in preserving civil good, and asserts that in this office the magistrate may please God. Secondly, the Mennonite Confession denies explicitly that Christians may be magistrates. This Confession of Smyth's is much more cautious and says that if the magistrate desires to follow Christ he may do so if he abandons all the powers and appurtenances of magistracy. This is saying the same as the Mennonite Confession, but it is putting the

[1] Smyth, *Works*, Articles 82–5.

whole position more cautiously, implicitly, negatively rather than positively. Smyth is clearly anxious that the spiritual kingdom of Christ should not encroach on the legitimate powers of the State. But if Smyth's Confession is implicit about Christians refusing the office of magistrate, and the Mennonites' explicit, on the subject of toleration Smyth is explicit, and the Waterlanders implicit. Church and State are separated in ends as well as in powers, and it has at last been appreciated that if religious liberty is to be secured, the State must concern itself with "only civil transgressions, injuries and wrongs".

In 1612 Smyth died at Amsterdam before even a section of his congregation had become united with the Waterlanders. Although the way to salvation was very strait and narrow to Smyth, he was not without the liberalism of a latitudinarian. In the Confession of 1609 he adopted Arminian principles, rejecting the rigid predestinarian doctrines of Calvin, giving, thereby, the early English Baptists their distinctive tenets compared with the Calvinist Baptists who emerge in 1640. It is true, however, that Smyth's Arminianism is of a different lineage from the doctrines of Arminius himself, and that neither Smyth nor the Mennonites were directly influenced by Arminian teachings.[1] In the covenant of his Gainsborough Separatist Church, Smyth (as indeed Robinson and Jacob were later to do in theirs) had sanctioned a progressive outlook in religion, as opposed to an absolute finality in theology, when he covenanted with God and his congregation to "walk in all his ways

[1] Whitley, Preface to *Works* of Smyth, p. cvii.

made known, or be made known unto us, according to our best endeavours".[1] Smyth was also an extreme religious individualist. In the Confession of 1610 he asserted that although such as are not converted "have need of the Scriptures, creatures and ordinances of the Church" to instruct and comfort them, yet the "new creature which is begotten of God needeth not the outward Scriptures, creatures or ordinances of the Church to support and help him". Nevertheless, the regenerate will use the Church for the gaining and supporting of others (as Christ was above the law but yet came under it for our sakes); "and so the outward Church and ordinances are necessary for all sorts of persons whatsoever".[2] These three articles almost abolish the visible Church altogether, and are an anticipation of the Quakers. "*The Last Book of John Smyth called the Retraction of his Errors, and the confirmation of the Truth*" testifies to Smyth's personal charity and tolerance, and how at the end of his life he desired an end of pointless and bitter controversies so that he might the more devote himself to matters of faith. Moreover, he professed "that differences in judgment for matter of circumstance, as are all things of the outward Church, shall not cause me to refuse the brotherhood of any penitent and faithful Christian whatsoever".[3]

In the course of the negotiations with the Mennonites

[1] Burgess, *op. cit.* p. 85. Barrow's covenant had been "of faithful people gathered unto Jesus Christ, ordered and governed by the rule of his word in all things so far as shall be revealed unto them".

[2] Smyth, *Works*: "Propositions and Conclusions", Articles 60–2.

[3] *Ibid.* II, 755.

differences of opinion appeared in Smyth's congregation which by 1610 had divided it into three main groups. The first group, that led by Smyth, being discontented with Smyth's se-baptism, succeeded, after his death, in uniting themselves with the Mennonites by acceptance of the Mennonite Confession. But it was precisely this that the second group, led by Thomas Helwys, refused to do. Helwys held Smyth's se-baptism to be perfect, and refuted the belief, which had made Smyth anxious to join the Mennonites, that elders must be ordained by elders. He was also unwilling to accept the Mennonite view of the magistrate's office as being unlawful to a Christian, to which Smyth had subscribed. The third and least important group was led by Leonard Busher, who was accused of holding an error about the incarnation of Christ.[1]

In 1612 Thomas Helwys and his small congregation, having decided that flight from persecution was unlawful, returned to London, and, at Spitalfields, formed the first Baptist congregation in England. Since his secession from Smyth, Helwys had written several works in justification of his position, but by the beginning of 1612 he had made no explicit statement on the subject of toleration. In an article on the magistracy in the *Declaration of Faith* of 1611, he had stated that "in all lawful administrations" the use of the sword of God by the magistrate was to be supported, but there is no definition or even indication of what these "lawful administrations" are, and the main emphasis of the

[1] Burgess, *op. cit.* 181. Whitley, Preface to *Works* of Smyth, p. cix.

article was placed on the permission to Christians to hold the magistrate's office, wherein Helwys had differed from Smyth.[1] In an *Advertisement or Admonition unto the congregation which men call New Fryelers in the Low Countries* (i.e. to the Amsterdam Mennonites) published in 1611 Helwys had insisted again that "magistracy doth not debar any from the Church of Christ", and that although magistracy is a holy ordinance of God yet we must obey in conscience only in that which is holy and good—but again with no further definition.[2] These works did, however, reveal Helwys' spiritual individualism. The *Declaration of Faith* of 1611 was prefaced by an attack on authority in the Church, particularly the authority of learned divines, as Calvin, Beza and Perkins, and a plea that the individual Christian may cure his own ignorance of God's truth (which ignorance "is sin and unpardonable without repentance") by the study of God's word enlightened by His spirit. It is no good reason to believe a truth because Calvin has said it is so, for then "you hold the glorious gospel of Christ in respect of persons". Men should be led by the Spirit of God to such truths as it leads them to, and Helwys pleads with learned teachers not to be so confident in their understandings which are frequently mere human traditions. He asserts, further,

---

[1] "A Declaration of Faith of English People remaining at Amsterdam in Holland", Article 24 in McGlothlin, *Baptist Confessions of Faith*.

[2] Quoted from Underhill, Introductory notice to "Persecution for Religion judged and condemned", p. 88, in *Tracts on Liberty of Conscience and Persecution*, published in 1846 by the Hanserd Knollys Society.

the layman's capacity for attaining knowledge of divine truth. Let a man but read the Scriptures with God's help, and long and tedious courses of study are not necessary.[1] In a letter of 12 March 1610 to the Mennonites at Amsterdam dealing with the question of the succession to the ministry, differences over which had led to the secession from Smyth, Helwys maintained that "whosoever shall now be stirred up by the same spirit" as John the Baptist "to preach the same word, and men thereby being converted, may, according to John his example, wash them with water, and who can forbid?" For to forbid would be "contrary to the liberty of the Gospel which is free for all men, at all times and in all places".[2] Helwys' rejection of Calvinist predestinarian doctrines was in part due to his feeling that it destroyed the sense of individual responsibility. Predestinarian doctrine "makes some despair utterly as thinking there is no grace for them and that God hath decreed their destruction. And it makes others desperately careless, holding that if God have decreed they shall be saved, then they shall be saved, and if God have decreed they shall be damned, they shall be damned and in a desperate carelessness run headlong into destruction."[3]

In 1612, however, just before his return to England, Helwys published *A Short Declaration of The Mistery of*

---

[1] Quoted from Burgess, *op. cit.* pp. 204–11.

[2] Letter from T. Helwys and others to Waterland Church at Amsterdam. Burrage, *op. cit.* II, 181.

[3] Helwys, *A Short and Plain proof by the word and works of God that God's decree is not the cause of man's sin or condemnation,* 1611. Passage here quoted from Burgess, *op. cit.* p. 222.

Iniquity in which he defended his position against the bishops, the Puritans and the Barrowists, and vigorously attacked the persecuting policy of the Anglican hierarchy. This was a fuller statement of the case for religious liberty than Smyth's and was written with some eloquence, though its style and manner (full of repetitions) bear evidence that Helwys was greatly overwrought.[1] In this work it becomes clear how the Baptists' idea of religious liberty is a logical derivation from their extreme Protestantism. Justification for Helwys is so much by faith, that the true visible Church must consist only of those who are regenerate, and have been received freely into the congregation by believer's baptism. It is, therefore, essential to separate from all ungodliness—even to excluding from the Church infants of the regenerate themselves, because without faith they cannot belong to Christ's visible kingdom.[2] Helwys regards this extreme separation from the ungodliness of the Church of England (which is the second beast written of in the Book of Revelation, as Rome is the first) as inherent in any degree of separation. If the baptism of England and Rome is valid, then all Separatists have committed the sin of schism and should reunite themselves with Rome. But if it is not valid, then the separation must be as complete as that of the Baptists themselves.[3] Now this belief in justification by regenerate faith led, as, indeed, it had in part with the Barrowists, to a belief in the necessity of a free

[1] Burgess, *op. cit.* p. 276.

[2] Helwys, *The Mistery of Iniquity*, p. 163. This work has just been published by the Baptist Historical Society in facsimile from the edition of 1612.   [3] *Ibid.* p. 156.

conversion. It is, writes Helwys, "an unjust thing" and a "cruel tyranny" to "force men's consciences in their religion to God, seeing that if they err they must pay the price of their transgression with the loss of their souls". The individual is responsible to God alone in spiritual matters, and no command of the King can rid him of this responsibility when he stands before the judgment seat of God. Even those whom the King might compel to walk in the true way would not be acceptable to God unless they "obeyed the truth in love, whom the love of God constraineth".[1] But the Baptist, unlike the Barrowist, and precisely because his separation was the more extreme, carried this belief to its logical conclusion. "Christ will have no man's life touched for his cause. If the Samaritans will not receive him he passeth by them." No sword of justice may smite any for refusing Christ,[2] and this applies to all men however erroneous their beliefs. "For men's religion to God is betwixt God and themselves; the King shall not answer for it, neither may the King be judge between God and man. Let them be heretics, Turks, Jews or whatsoever it appertains not to the earthly power to punish them in the least."[3] Church and State are therefore to be separated in ends as well as powers. No sword of justice is to be used "to keep in obedience the people of God and the King to the laws, statutes and ordinances of Christ which appertain to the well governing of his kingdom", for the sword of Christ's kingdom is spiritual only, by the power of which "Christ's subjects are to be ruled and kept in obedience".[4] "God hath given our

[1] *Ibid.* p. 46.   [2] *Ibid.* p. 47.   [3] *Ibid.* p. 69.   [4] *Ibid.* p. 48.

lord the King all earthly power which extendeth to all the goods and bodies of his servants", but hath reserved for Himself His heavenly kingdom.[1] Neither kings nor "spiritual lords" (i.e. bishops) can have coercive power over the Church because "they are mortal men and not God".[2] For the King or "spiritual lords" to demand unquestioning obedience to their religious decrees is an assumption of infallibility; "for if the King's people must not believe that they only (i.e. the bishops) have the power of the spirit and cannot err, how comes it that the King's people must be compelled only to obey them in all their understandings and practices, except the King's people must obey them though they do err?"[3] Moreover if Christian kings are given power in matter of religion then all heathen and heretic princes possess it too, "for all earthly powers are one and the same in their several dominions".[4] Helwys emphasizes that to the Baptist this question of the government of the Church is absolutely fundamental, since it concerns the sufficiency of Christ's power in His own kingdom, and that it is not, as the Puritan would make it, a thing comparatively indifferent.[5] For him a ruling presbytery "is but old priest writ large". "For if a ruling presbytery by their synodal decrees and ordinances be lawful, then why not a ruling prelacy by convocation, canons lawful; and why not a ruling Pope?"[6]

Compared with that of Smyth, Helwys' position in

---

[1] Helwys, *The Mistery of Iniquity*, pp. 40–1.
[2] *Ibid.* Inscription to King James written on fly leaf of copy preserved in Bodleian.
[3] *Ibid.* p. 64.   [4] *Ibid.* p. 43.
[5] *Ibid.* pp. 109–13.   [6] *Ibid.* p. 102.

face of the claims of the State is stronger, and he is as anxious that the Church should not interfere in purely temporal matters as he is that the State should not interfere with matters of conscience.[1] He allows the magistrate to be a Christian, though as a member of the Church he is subject to spiritual censures.[2] These spiritual censures, however, do not constitute an encroachment by the Church on the rights of the State, because he had already laid it down in the Confession of 1611 that "excommunicants in respect of civil society are not to be avoided".[3] He is quick, moreover, to repudiate that difference in religion means sedition against the State, and he makes it clear that if the magistrate does transgress the integrity of the Church, Christians "are not to resist by any way or means although it were in their power, but rather to submit to give their lives, as Christ and his disciples did, and yet keep their consciences to God".[4] By this fuller recognition of the legitimate powers of the State, Helwys did something to free the English Baptists from the charge of being anarchists which had for long, not without justification, been levelled at the continental Anabaptists.[5]

[1] *Ibid.* p. 39.   [2] *Ibid.* p. 48.
[3] Helwys, *Confession* of 1611, Article 18.
[4] Helwys, *The Mistery of Iniquity*, p. 83.
[5] Henry Burton in *For God and King*, 1636, classed Papists and Anabaptists together as conceding too little power to magistracy. Edmund Jessop, who at one time was an Anabaptist himself, in *A Discovery of the Errors of the English Anabaptists*, 1623, wrote that "though the view that the magistrate cannot be a true Christian except he give over his magistracy is not fully the opinion of the English Anabaptists" yet it is held by other Anabaptists; and even the English "are not rightly informed as to the authority of the magistrate".

There is, however, no trace of the latitudinarian in Helwys, as there had been in Smyth. The gates of the kingdom of heaven are open but narrowly in his eyes. Few men shall be saved, since most live under the power of the beast,[1] and he complains of those less strict Separatists who "make the way broad and wide which God hath made strait and narrow".[2] Nor is he willing to admit that those who err through ignorance and defend their error are capable of salvation.[3] And although he had pleaded eloquently for the right of the individual to search Scripture for himself, he shows himself on more than one occasion incapable of realizing that there can be any other honest interpretation than his own.[4]

By 1613 Helwys was certainly imprisoned in London and very probably dead.[5] In 1614, however, Leonard Busher, who had led the third division of Smyth's original congregation, but who had returned to England with Helwys, published an even fuller plea for religious liberty and an attack on persecution entitled *Religions Peace: or A plea for Liberty of Conscience*. That this should have been the earliest pamphlet in England to devote itself wholly to arguing the cause of religious liberty is a testimony of the increasing importance that toleration was assuming in Baptist eyes. No doubt the persecution in England, which Helwys and Busher had deliberately returned from the security of the Low Countries to face, was in part responsible for this, but

---

[1] Helwys, *The Mistery of Iniquity*, p. 12.
[2] *Ibid*. p: 181.   [3] *Ibid*. p. 192.
[4] *Ibid*. p. 197.   [5] Burrage, *op. cit.* 1, 256.

as time went on Smyth's original hesitancy over the lawfulness of magistracy was replaced by an increasingly full appreciation of the importance of toleration as part of the logic of the Baptist position.

Religions Peace, however, premises Baptist principles implicitly, and incidentally, rather than explicitly. Its method is to present certain arguments against persecution and then to draw conclusions as to the relation between Church and State, and the policy which the King ought to follow in the existing situation.[1] True religion, first, can come only by faith and regeneration, for Christ said: "Except a man be born again he cannot see the kingdom of God." As God only can command faith, and as His kingdom is not of this world, so in spiritual matters spiritual weapons only can be efficacious, and therefore as the true religion is attained by the word and spirit of God, so should it be defended. Secondly, persecution is in any case against Christ's merciful law. Christ Himself, who came to save not to destroy, for the conversion not for the destruction of sinners, never used constraint, and commanded His disciples only to preach to all nations and baptize them, and if they were repulsed, to do no more than shake the dust off their feet. He taught, too, that men should do as they would be done by, and that the wheat and the tares must both be suffered together until the harvest. Thirdly, therefore, to persecute the tares before their

[1] The pamphlet is not very systematic, and tends to repeat itself. In my analysis of it, therefore, in order to give a greater coherence, I have rearranged it into a more logical order of my own. It should be said, however, that it is more systematic and more clearly thought out than most pamphlets of the same period.

time is not only against Christ's command, but is a usurpation of His judgment seat. Persecution may lead to the persecution of Christ in true Christians, for Scripture foretells that although true Christians may be persecuted, yet they themselves never persecute.[1] But, fourthly, persecution is never in any case really successful. It hinders the conversion of the Jews, of unbelievers, of the unrepentant. It encourages others to persecute, and condemns persecution in those who themselves condemn persecution in others (as Protestants condemning the persecution carried out by the Papists and yet persecuting others themselves, condemn their own practice thereby). And if persecution is never successful, still less is it necessary. Unless persecution is to be allowed to make shipwreck of faith by forcing a religion on men against their consciences, they must try the spirits, whether they be of God, and hear all doctrines. Nor is it dangerous to expose erroneous doctrines to those who hitherto may not have been aware of them. For "you shall understand that errors being brought to the light of the word of God, will vanish as darkness before the light of a torch. Even as the chaff before the wind cannot stand, so error before truth cannot abide. Therefore it is no hindrance but a great furtherance to have all erroneous rocks in the haven to heaven made known and published." Fifthly, persecution is dangerous to the safety and welfare of the State. Persecution breeds hypocrisy, and hypocrisy traitors to God and the King. Forced consciences cause plots, and Busher cites the case of Digby, Catesby and Percy, the traitors

[1] This is proved at length from Revelation xvii. 3–6.

126

of the Gunpowder Plot, who would never have been so had not their consciences been forced. Persecution is a danger to both prince and people, whereas permission of conscience is not only a furtherance to the Gospel but a safety to both, as the experience of Holland and England under Elizabeth has shown. Great trade and commerce, too, would ensue through the Jews and others who now are driven elsewhere. Finally, to bring the matter home to the King, to whom, together with Parliament, the pamphlet was addressed, Busher urges that as King and Parliament would not themselves be forced by the Pope, so ought not they to force other men's consciences.

The consequences which Busher draws from this repudiation of persecution may be divided into theoretical and practical. Of the theoretical the first concerns the nature of the visible Church. No Church, according to Busher, which uses the sword to force all men into it, whether they be regenerate Christians or not, can be a true Church. In order to prevent the use of force in religious matters Church and State must be separated in ends as well as in powers. "Kings are to rule temporal affairs by the sword of their temporal kingdoms, and bishops and ministers are to rule spiritual affairs by the word and spirit of God, the sword of Christ's spiritual kingdom, and not to meddle with one another's authority, office and function." Kings may be Christians and yet retain their magistracy, and be given "by the laws of God all earthly honour, fear and reverence" and be paid "willingly tribute and custom, tax and toll so much and so often as it shall please his majesty and Parliament to appoint and gather, by an officer or officers whatsoever". The King and Parliament, therefore, "may please to permit all sorts of Christians; yea Jews, Turks and Pagans, so long as they are peaceable and no malefactors..., which if they be, let them be punished according to God's word". Jews, Christians, Turks are all tolerated at Constantinople. "If this be so how much more ought Christians not to force one another to religion? And how much more ought Christians to tolerate Christians, whereas Turks do tolerate them?"

The practical conclusions and proposals of Busher begin by placing the responsibility for the persecuting policy of the Anglican Church, which has made it a false Church, upon the bishops. He condemns their spiritual lordships, which usurp the title of Christ, their revenues and their state, and asks whether the persecution of the martyrs under Queen Mary was not due to bishops. Moreover, it is a serious question for the King to consider what would happen were he to differ in religion from that established by law in the land (as Elizabeth did in Mary's days), particularly if the matter were in the hands of the bishops. Shall he too be constrained and persecuted as Elizabeth was by Mary?[1] The King, therefore, should realize that, as he may lawfully be a Christian and yet retain the magistracy, so he must consider himself the minister of God, and not the minister of the bishops. In the existing situation the King thus comes to have certain duties. As Antichrist

[1] Busher does admit that the bishops persecute in zeal for God, but emphasizes that learning is not wisdom.

first rose by the power of Kings, so shall she be put down. "As she had her exaltation and arrival to the height and dignity of the see empire of Rome by the love of Kings...so shall she have her consummation and abolition from that height and dignity, by the hatred of Kings, who again shall take their power and authority from her, and therewith defend the peace and persons of the saints and servants of Jesus; and now for religion's peace, will use their power and authority against the bloody persecution of Anti-Christ, and all his bloody bishops and ministers, and so become nursing fathers unto the Church of Christ."[1] Busher therefore contemplates the fall of Antichrist at the King's hand simply by his withdrawal of the civil power which he had previously lent to her, and he constantly emphasizes that if liberty of conscience were established, the power of the bishops would fall to the ground, as error before the word of God. Nevertheless, Busher does say that if the bishops will not confess their idolatrous estate, then they "ought to be pulled down and suppressed like the abbots, their lordly brethren; though not sacrificed unto the Lord in Smithfield, as the godly King Josiah sacrificed the idol priests of the high places on the altars thereof". For the King may also use the civil power he has withdrawn from Antichrist to defend religion's peace against those who disturb it by persecution. "The King and State may defend religion's peace by their sword and civil power, but not the faith, other than by the word and spirit of God." This is perhaps the most important sentence in the whole pamphlet.

[1] This from an interpretation of Revelation xvii. 12–18.

Further, though Christ has freed us from the ecclesiastical laws of the Old Testament yet the King still should execute the moral and judicial law of God—which is a law of love and doing as one would be done by.

To prevent any danger to the safety of the State from these proposals Busher lays down certain rules which should accompany permission of conscience. Most of these concern the distinguishing and disarming of persons tainted with treason, but he also provides that no disputants should resort to violence, and that there should be complete freedom of writing and publishing for all sects, provided Scripture only is used as a proof of their contentions. The significance of this latter condition will appear hereafter. If the proposals he suggests were to be carried out great peace and prosperity would ensue; but if they are rejected he comforts the persecuted with the reflection that God will triumph in the end.

Now the question immediately arises how far the duties that Busher ascribes to the King constitute, in themselves, a violation of the separation of Church and State. From the view-point of a Baptist, permission to the King to suppress the office of bishop and its Popish laws and canons, clearly does not constitute an unlawful exercise of the use of the civil power, and in this connection the analogy Busher draws to Henry VIII's suppression of the abbots is important. For the Anglicans themselves would have agreed that the suppression of the abbots was not an interference with the Church by the State, but a reclamation by the State of secular jurisdiction over certain persons and causes that had eluded this lawful extent of the State's boundaries. Busher merely wants to carry this process further and to abolish bishops and their coercive jurisdiction, which, for him, are not parts of the true Church at all, and who therefore, as persecutors disturbing religion's peace, may legitimately be dealt with by the civil power. With this, of course, the Anglican would have disagreed (for many, following Bancroft, believed that episcopacy was *jure divino*) as the Roman Catholic had disagreed in the case of the abbots, claiming it to be an unlawful violation of the Church by the State. From the Roman Catholic point of view the suppression of the abbots did, indeed, constitute such a violation, as the suppression of bishops would from the view-point of the Anglican; but to the Baptist neither of these would constitute a violation of the Church, because he held a different conception of the nature of the true visible Church. But if this is so, is the morality of the Baptist in these matters really superior to that of the Anglican? Is he not also, as would the Anglican, prohibiting the Prince from hindering what he conceives to be true religion, and permitting him to use his civil power against the contrary, on the grounds that it is no part of the true Church? From the point of view of toleration, the Baptist is superior, precisely because of his conception of the nature of the Church; and the power which Busher here gives to the King is a civil power to prevent the bishops from maintaining their position by other weapons than their adversaries possess. He envisages no persecution of the bishops' persons; he allows them complete freedom to express and maintain their beliefs; but he does wish the King to prohibit them from proceeding against their adversaries by the use of civil force or by that power which comes from worldly wealth. The bishops in exercising coercive authority were usurping the power of the State as well as violating the rights of the Church, and Busher's plea is that the separation may be made absolute, for only then can liberty of conscience be established. It would be fatal to misconstrue liberty of conscience into meaning liberty to force one's beliefs upon others, and Busher's permission to the King to "defend religion's peace, but not the faith other than by the word and spirit of God" is, therefore, not an approximation to the political theory of the latitudinarian, but a necessary condition of any liberty of conscience which is to be secured by the separation of Church and State, for neither authority can be allowed to usurp the power or end of the other. Whether Busher was justified in including the wealth of the bishops under the same usurpation as their exercise of civil force is, of course, more questionable. For although he clearly considered that the power thence derived was illegitimately used to enforce conscience, he is also unmistakably actuated by theological hatred.

Nevertheless, Busher's belief in absolute truth, known and ascertained, did lead him into one serious mitigation of his liberty of conscience. He is prepared to allow freedom of the press to all sects provided that they only use God's word in proof of their contentions. Now, in effect, this is to deny liberty of the press to Roman Catholics, because it was in the essence of their position to base their defence on other authorities than Scripture. This Busher evidently realized because he proceeds to say with some satisfaction, that as a result of this proposed regulation "both few errors and few books will be written seeing all false ministers have little else besides the Fathers to build their religion upon". Error will not then be written save by obstinate persons and seared consciences, seeing that God's word is no shelter for error. In some sense this mitigation of liberty of conscience (Busher would probably not have recognized it as such) is more unconscious than deliberate, but it is a good example of the sort of inconsistency to which the belief in an absolute truth (and that a revealed one) constantly leads the separatist tolerationist, and how liberty of conscience is after all less fundamental in his life than we shall see it is in that of the latitudinarian.[1]

In 1615 John Murton, who had returned to England with Helwys and had become leader of his congregation after the death of Helwys sometime before 1616, published a further tract on liberty of conscience entitled *Objections: Answered by way of Dialogue, wherein is proved, by the law of God, by the law of our land, by his Majesties testimonies; That no man ought to be persecuted for his religion, so he testify his allegiance by the Oath appointed by the Law*. The very title and form of this pamphlet are significant, and that it is a consideration of a series of objections against liberty of conscience shows that since the publication of *Religions Peace* the problem

[1] *Religions Peace* is included in the *Tracts on Liberty of Conscience* published during the last century by the Hanserd Knollys Society. It should be noted that Busher does also admit as true Christians all who confess Jesus the Messiah.

of persecution had been further debated in Baptist minds, and that this was the reply to the objections raised by sects less tolerant than they.

Objections: Answered, however, covers little ground that had not already been considered in *Religions Peace*. All arguments against liberty of conscience based on the Old Testament are rejected because the order in the Kingdom of Israel was merely a carnal "figure and type" of the spiritual kingdom of Christ, who in fulfilling the law thereby abolished it. As for texts ostensibly favouring persecution drawn from the New Testament, Murton not only rejects and repudiates them on circumstantial grounds, but quotes also a long list of Christ's merciful testimonies. In the case of Ananias and Sapphira, as also of Elymas the sorcerer, for example, Murton asserts that Paul did not directly condemn them, but only decreed God's judgment against them, the execution thereof being left to the Deity Himself. As for the text "Compel them to come in", Murton admits its validity provided compulsion be with the word of God only and not with the sword. With the whip in the Temple Christ fulfilled the carnal law of the Old Testament, and thereby abolished it. The suggestion that liberty of conscience may be dangerous to King and State, or that by breeding divisions it may bring sedition, is repudiated at some length. Murton sensibly admits that Christ "who is the Prince of peace, not of sedition, hath taught that he came not to send peace on the earth but debate"; and his desire is that the fire of such sedition shall be kindled. But that this difference in religion should bring civil dissensions Murton denies, for "behold the nations where freedom of religion is permitted, and you may see that there are not more flourishing or prosperous nations under the heavens than they are". The King has repeatedly written (and Murton quotes his writings) that he desires to punish no one for conscience' sake, and that he will be satisfied with the Oath of Allegiance. Murton expresses himself satisfied with this, if the King would only carry it out, and agrees that all those who refuse the Oath of Allegiance should be dealt with at the King's pleasure. The Reformers are not seditious like Papists, though he admits that Papists are largely driven to seditious practices because of their forced consciences. But if magistrates are to be obeyed absolutely in all earthly things, yet with "all men they must let God alone with his right", and recognize that they must respect the rights of the subject as subjects respect the rights of the Prince. Thus, if princes are freed from any obligation to excommunicated subjects (as Murton thinks they are not) then why should not subjects be freed from all obligation to excommunicated princes? If, in other words, it is justifiable for a prince to punish those excommunicated from what he regards to be the true Church by the civil sword (as all Separatists were excommunicated by the Canons of 1604), it is equally justifiable for subjects to seek the deposition of a prince excommunicated from a church which they believe to be true. It is therefore illogical of the bishops at once to condemn the doctrine of deposition and tyrannicide (which they do rightly), and at the same time to urge the persecution by the civil power of those who differ from them in religion (which is wrong). For thereby they cry out against tyrannicide and yet justify it, by urging princes to murder their subjects for precisely the same reason as Papists preach tyrannicide—being contrary minded in religion. It follows, then, that if tyrannicide is a wicked doctrine, so too must be persecution of subjects for mere difference in religion.

For the rest, Murton's pamphlet uses all the arguments that we have already seen in *Religions Peace*. Like Busher, Murton places the responsibility for the persecuting policy of the Anglican Church upon the bishops, who are the second beast spoken of in the Book of Revelation, for the King is "no bloodthirsty man", as may be seen from comparing the restraint he exercises upon the bishops with the exercise of the power of this spiritual beast under Henry VIII after the separation from Rome. Nevertheless, the present King does give his power to "the spiritual beast of England, which sets up a worship, as they pretend, of God, and force all thereto by civil persecutions". The bishops tolerate any man in their Church, however sinful, and punish every one without it, however good—which is wholly to misinterpret the parable of the tares and wheat being left together until the harvest. For the field in which both were sown means the world, in which all men, however sinful, must be tolerated, and not the Church, out of which all sinners must be cast, unless they repent, by the power of excommunication. Precisely because the bishops (in the Court of High Commission for example) proceed not against sinners within the Church, but against those without it over whom they have no power, and that, not by the ultimate power of excommunication, but by the civil force of the magistrate, Murton pleads with the King to put down this Antichrist, as by his power it arose. The beast, however, is to be put down merely, as Busher had urged, by the King withdrawing his civil power from the bishops, who not only use it for an unlawful end, but thereby also usurp the magistrate's power. The King himself has stated that as the kings of the earth support the power of the beast, so by their power shall it be taken away. If the King would but follow his own words "and take but his own, their titles of greatness and forms of honouring them, and their temporal livings this spiritual power would stand very naked and desolate".

It is thus that Murton and Busher have both proceeded from a simple separation of Church and State into a closer examination of what constitutes matter of State, and what matter of Religion. In their demand either for the bishops to abandon their abuse of the civil power, or for the King to withdraw it from them, using it against their persecuting policy to defend "religion's peace", they were asking no more than the circumstances required if liberty of conscience were to be established. As for Murton's recognition that Roman Catholics who refuse the Oath of Allegiance may legitimately be left at the disposal of the King, it is an acquiescence in persecution of a sort (though Murton would certainly not have recognized it as such), but a persecution which may equally well be regarded as a legitimate protection of the State against possible traitors whose practices might lead not merely to civil disorder but possibly to civil war. As we have mentioned before, this is not to deny that any Roman Catholics who suffered thereby were martyrs to their faith, but it is to recognize that, the demands of the State in the light of the Gunpowder Plot being such as were simply necessary for its continued preservation, and the beliefs of certain Roman Catholics being such as they were, the conflict between the two was inevitable and insoluble, so long as these two factors remained constant.[1] It is impossible, indeed, to blame either party, because both were doing what, from their own point of view, must be recognized as legitimate. Moreover, it should not be forgotten that had the Roman Catholics who refused the Oath of Allegiance gained power in the period at present under consideration there would have been a holocaust of their opponents far more terrible than the persecution of James (though this admittedly raises the nice question, which we cannot answer here, as to whether it is legitimate, believing in liberty of conscience, to sacrifice it temporarily in order that, in the long period, it may be preserved).

Murton concludes *Objections: Answered* by a consideration of what the true Christian ought to do in face of the persecuting policy of the bishops, supposing liberty of conscience is not established. In practice this amounts to a defence of his Baptist beliefs against the Familists,[2] the Presbyterians, the Independents, the

[1] The clause requiring the condemnation of the deposing power as heretical, was, as has been seen, less defensible, though, with James' gloss on it, it was much less oppressive than most Papists were inclined to make out.

[2] For an account of the tenets of the Family of Love in relation to the idea of toleration see Appendix.

Barrowists, and the remnant, even, of Smyth's Baptist congregation in Amsterdam who were just about to unite with the Mennonites, and whom Murton condemns for fleeing from persecution.[1]

The quotation by Murton of King James' testimony against persecution for cause of conscience was the first occasion on which Baptists had supplemented Scriptural by human authority. In 1620, however, in *A Most Humble Supplication of many of the King's Majesty's loyal subjects ready to testify all civil obedience by the Oath of Allegiance or otherwise, and that of conscience, who are persecuted (only for differing in religion) contrary to divine and human testimonies* Murton carried this practice further and supported his argument by extensive quotation from the Fathers, the sayings of foreign princes, and the partial testimonies of other religious sects who were interested in toleration for themselves alone. The earlier part of this *Supplication* was concerned with proving that the practice of the bishops belied their own theory when they insisted upon obedience to the commands of the Church as such, and yet taught that the Scriptures only are the rule of faith. Murton urged that as "the rule of faith is the doctrine of the Holy Ghost contained in the sacred Scriptures, and not any Church, Council, Prince, or Potentate, nor any mortal man whatsoever", so "the spirit of God to understand and interpret the Scriptures is given to all and every particular person that fear and obey God of what degree soever they be". "Those that fear and obey God",

[1] *Objections: Answered* is also included in *Tracts on Liberty of Conscience.*

moreover, "and so have the spirit of God to search out and know the mind of God in the Scriptures, are commonly and for the most part, the simple, poor, despised", and "the learned in human learning do commonly err, and know not the truth, but persecute it, and the professors of it; and therefore are no further to be followed" than in so far as they agree with the truth. Murton sought to prove this by Biblical and patristic authority, and then proceeded to demonstrate that "persecution for cause of conscience is not only against the doctrine of Jesus Christ", but "is against the profession and practice of famous princes", and "is condemned by the ancient and later writers, yea by Puritans and Papists". He quotes the testimonies of King James, Stephen, King of Poland and of Frederick, Elector Palatine, King of Bohemia; of Hilary, Tertullian, Jerome, Brentius, Luther, the Puritan Supplication of 1609, and even a "wicked" but unspecified Papist book "lately set forth". For the rest Murton contended, as he had in *Obiections: Answered* that liberty of conscience would in no way prejudice the Commonwealth, but on the contrary would make it flourish, and that kings who maintain such a liberty are not thereby deprived of any of the power given them of God, for the King of Israel is now Christ who has all spiritual power to govern His Church. Church and State must therefore be separated in ends as well as powers. The King is "lord and lawgiver to the bodies of his subjects, and all belonging to their outward man, for the preservation of himself and his good subjects and for the punishment of evil. In which preservation the Church of Christ hath a special part when their outward peace is thereby preserved from the fury of all adversaries; in which respect princes are called nursing fathers" (i.e. the Prince's power extends to defending "religion's peace"). But unto God we must give the things that are God's "which is to be Lord and Lawgiver to the soul in that spiritual worship and service which he requireth"; and with these no Prince may interfere. "You may not add nor diminish" God's laws; "they are perfect already; nor be judge nor monarch of his Church" for "that is Christ's right".

Historically this is perhaps the most important of the Baptist considerations on religious liberty, because several years later it was to provoke a reply and a counter-reply by John Cotton and Roger Williams respectively which examined, with a systematic thoroughness lacking in these early Baptist works, the whole problem of the separation of Church and State.[1] As far as can be gathered the Baptist pleas for religious liberty made little impression on English people,[2] and were probably forgotten (if, indeed, they were ever noticed) almost as soon as they were published, although in the period of acute controversy over toleration during the Civil War and the Commonwealth, *Religions Peace* was reprinted again in 1646 by Henry Burton, and in 1662 *Objections: Answered* was republished under the title of *Persecution for Religion Judged and Condemned*.[3]

---

[1] *The Bloody Tenent of Persecution* by R. Williams, published in 1644.   [2] Burrage, *op. cit.* I, 259.
[3] *Vide* introductory notice to such of these pamphlets as are included in *Tracts on Liberty of Conscience* by Underhill.

After 1624 the history of Baptism in England becomes very obscure until the emergence of the Calvinist or Particular Baptists at the opening of the Civil War. Baptists of the General or Arminian type undoubtedly survived in scattered congregations, but there are no more pleas for religious liberty. Indeed, after 1625, with the change of King and the growing influence of Laud, there is a marked diminution of polemical literature amongst sectarians of all kinds on the subject of toleration. It is, however, known that the original congregation of Helwys, to whose spiritual leadership John Murton had succeeded, excommunicated Elias Tookey and sixteen others. These applied for reception into the Waterlander Mennonite Church at Amsterdam, and their correspondence with the Waterlanders survives in the Mennonite archives. Tookey, whose union with the Mennonites was never consummated, met with much the same difficulties which had caused Helwys to break with Smyth. He and his congregation resolutely refused to condemn magistracy, the use of the oath and war as unlawful in civil causes, because this would take away all government amongst men, though they equally strongly disallowed them in spiritual causes. If they were to condemn these institutions (as the Mennonites wanted them to) they pointed out how difficult would be their position in England, where it was essential to take the Oath of Allegiance. At first (in a letter by Tookey of 3 January 1624) they so far conceded to the Mennonite position over magistracy and the profession of arms as to say that they will "neither take nor assume one of them", but later they emphatically refused any absolute condemnation. A further impediment to the desired union were the opinions of certain members of Tookey's congregation about the Deity of Christ. "Further we inform you that there is nobody amongst us who denies the deity of Christ; but there are two or three who have a somewhat different opinion than we maintain in general, though we think that after all it comes to the same end."[1] Although, therefore, these Baptists show no clear trace of holding or tolerating in their Church Socinian opinions, there is no doubt that, as in the case of Leonard Busher, Socinian influences are making themselves felt. Tookey further maintained that although there are differences amongst them about the Deity of Christ yet "we can bear with each other in peace", and the belief is expressed "that such Christian tolerance" is a better preservation against discord in the Church than "minute examinations, limitations, censures and condemnations only for opinion".[2] A wise observation, and one from which most sectarians could have profited.

[1] Tookey to Mennonites from London 3 January 1624. Burgess, *op. cit.* pp. 328 *seq.*
[2] Tookey to Mennonites, 17 March 1625. Burgess, *op. cit.* pp. 328 *seq.*

CHAPTER VI

THE THEORY OF THE ANGLICAN
LATITUDINARIAN DIVINES

THE intellectual perplexity of the early seventeenth century (which Donne's sonnet so aptly expressed in its theological aspect), served, as has been seen, not to disillusion those of Puritan or Separatist mentality, whence emerged the first type of tolerationist, but rather to impress upon them the necessity of carrying Protestant principles to their logical conclusion, by seeking further reformation or separating wholly from all pollutions. If the Reformation had not succeeded, to them it was because there had not been reform enough. But to those who possessed the mentality which characterizes the second type of tolerationist (and they included all the finer minds of the age) such further extremes of fanaticism were of no assistance. For them truth was not so easily ascertained, nor, when tentatively arrived at, so easily confirmed by reference to an infallible authority. The claims of infallible authorities were, as a swift solution to their intellectual difficulties, to some of them their greatest temptation, but the rejection of these claims in favour of reason was in all cases the source of their intellectual strength. The development of latitudinarian thought on toleration takes place, on the whole, during the second part of the period which is at present under consideration, during the reign of Charles I and under the doctrinally tolerant regime of Laud.

In this chapter we shall consider the theory of those writers who approached and arrived at the latitudinarian position from a specifically theological angle. From the time of Elizabeth's settlement of the Church the best Anglican thought, even amongst the ruling authorities of the Church itself, had never adopted a position of narrow doctrinal rigidity. Both Hooker and Donne had combined the Anglican justification of persecution with a considerable approximation to the full latitudinarian position, and Laud himself had rejected the doctrine of exclusive salvation and regarded doctrinal disputes tolerantly, provided they did not disturb the peace of the Church. Now the latitudinarian necessarily approaches the idea of toleration through a growing belief in the importance of doctrinal tolerance, and in the period under consideration there were not wanting divines to whom the necessity for charity and doctrinal tolerance appeared so urgent that they may be said to have become full latitudinarian tolerationists. Like Laud these thinkers condemned the doctrine of exclusive salvation, but they also went further and implicitly condemned Laud's practice by their insistence upon unity not being identical with uniformity, and by their belief in the necessity for freedom in all except the few fundamentals which they conceived to be necessary for salvation. Archbishop Ussher insisted that the true Church should admit into her communion all who willingly professed the name of Christ and demand no other qualification.[1]

[1] In *A briefe declaration of the universalitie of the Church of Christ.*

Bishop Hall explained the reason for this position when he urged that faith and not form is the principal element in Christian unity, and that faith can consist of nothing more than the few fundamentals which are necessary to salvation.[1] Heresy therefore is a rare sin, and usually should be treated with spiritual rather than temporal weapons.[2] Some even whose sympathies were Puritan rather than Arminian were coming to similar conclusions. Richard Sibbes so believed in the necessity for charity and compassion that he condemned the insistence upon so many fundamentals as necessary to salvation, and Thomas Scott, who believed that all Protestants at least were united on all essential doctrines, urged that unity could only be achieved by the exercise of a larger tolerance and a more comprehensive charity.[3]

The fullest statement of the latitudinarian position in this period approached from a specifically theological angle, however, is to be found in the works of John Hales and of William Chillingworth, and these we shall examine in detail as the clearest formulation of the latitudinarian beliefs which were coming to be held by many reasonable men as the best solution to the problem which Donne's sonnet had posed.

[1] Hall, "On Unity", *Works*, v, 282.
[2] Hall, *Works*, vi, 649.
[3] For a fuller examination of the theories of these minor latitudinarians see Jordan, *The Development of Religious toleration in England*, 1603–40, pp. 143–57 and 358–63.

I

JOHN HALES OF ETON

The ever memorable Mr John Hales of Eton was an unwearied seeker after truth. Hales was a member of Ben Jonson's literary circle, and it was he that Sir John Suckling playfully urged to "leave Socinus and the Schoolmen" at Eton, and to come to town where his friends might enjoy his company.[1] He was also one of Lord Falkland's company at Great Tew. In his pursuit of truth, to which his letter to Laud so movingly testifies,[2] Hales, the earliest rational theologian of the seventeenth century,[3] adopted as his guiding principle "reason illuminated by revelation out of God's word".[4] In a sermon, *Of Enquiry and Private Judgment in Religion*, Hales rejected all infallible authorities and insisted that the only infallible judge in controversies of faith must be each individual for himself. For a man must not only know what he believes, but why he believes it also; because there is no other way to God "but by thoroughly perceiving and understanding religion, and discovering the uttermost grounds on which it subsists". When men put off the responsibility for their

[1] See also the stanza on Hales in Suckling's *Session of the Poets*. Aubrey describes Hales as a "pretty little man, sanguine, of a cheerful countenance, very gentle and courteous".

[2] Hales, J., *Works*, I, 135, ed. 1756. (A letter to Archbishop Laud upon the occasion of the "Tract concerning schism").

[3] Throughout this chapter I owe a general debt to Tulloch, *Rational Theology in England*.

[4] Hales, *Works*, I: "Tract on the Sacrament of the Lord's Supper and concerning the Church mistaking itself about fundamentals."

religion upon other authorities, it is ultimately fallible human authority in some form which they trust. Nor is it a virtue to esteem our reason as meaner than that of others. To advice and counsel we must modestly listen, but completely to abandon our own faculties is "poverty of spirit and indiscretion". Such reliance upon the individual reason may, indeed, breed contentions and disquiet, but it is wrong to purchase our own peace by "nourishing a still humour in others" (as the Sybarites, to procure their ease, banished their smiths, because their trade was full of noise), for "that peace which ariseth out of ignorance is but a kind of sloth, a moral lethargy seeming quiet, because it hath no power to move".[1]

It follows from this that Hales believed in the importance of following conscience in all circumstances. "It is a fearful thing to trifle with conscience, for most assuredly, according unto it, a man shall stand or fall at the last." It is true "the exception of a good conscience sounds not well with many men, because oft-times under that form pertinacy and wilfulness is suspected to couch itself", but in this case it merely concerns a man the more "sincerely to know the truth of his own heart, and so accordingly to determine his own way, whatever the judgment of his superiors be or whatsoever event befall him".[2] This insistence upon what would now be called intellectual honesty is a marked feature of Hales' work. In the "Tract concerning Schism and Schismatics" Hales asserts that the individual will be well able to judge when a necessary separation becomes an un-

[1] Hales, *Works*, III.   [2] *Ibid.* vol. I, letter to Laud.

JOHN HALES

necessary schism "if so you be animo defoecato, if you have cleared yourself from froth and grounds; if neither sloth, nor fears, nor ambition, nor any tempting spirit of that nature abuse you (for these, and such as these, are the true impediments why both that and other questions of the like danger are not truly answered)".[1]

Not unconnected with this insistence upon intellectual honesty in following conscience, is Hales' protest against the tendency of the age to make the test of a man's justification in the eyes of God a mere willingness to accept a creed postulating certain intellectual beliefs, to the neglect of the real morality of his life. "I must confess that I have not yet made that proficiency in the schools of our age, as that I could see, why the second table and the acts of it are not as properly parts of religion and Christianity as the acts and observations of the first." Provided their beliefs be honestly held, men of widely differing creeds may all do God glory in different ways, for it is "the unity of the spirit in the bond of peace" and not "identity of conceit which the Holy Ghost requires at the hands of Christians". As an instance of this Hales cites the Arminian-Calvinist controversy. The "will of God and his manner of proceeding in predestination is indiscernible" and both the Arminian and the Calvinist view may, with equal "probability of Scripture", be held.[2] "Were we not ambitiously minded, everyone to be the lord of a sect,

[1] *Ibid.* vol. I.

[2] Hales was in a good position to appreciate this because though formerly a Predestinarian-Calvinist, he later became an Arminian. *Vide infra.*

each of these tenets might be profitably taught and heard, and matter of singular exhortation drawn from them."[1]

In his application of these principles to the problems whence persecution proceeds, Hales everywhere insists that the violent controversies, schisms, heresies, and separations in Christendom are always the result of unreasonable and uncharitable behaviour. "One very potent and strong" cause of these divisions "is the exceeding affection and love unto our own conceits. For grown we are unto extremities on both hands, we cannot with patience either admit of other men's opinions, or endure that our own should be withstood." And certainly, "scarcely can there be found a thing more harmful to religion than to vent thus our own conceits, and obtrude them upon the world for necessary and absolute". Some men, for example, "deal with Scripture as chimics deal with natural bodies, torturing them to extract that out of them which God and nature never put in them". But when "we contend not for the authority of Scripture but for the authority of our own interpretations...then are we guilty of this great sin of wresting Scripture". Hales therefore insists that only "the literal, plain and uncontroversable meaning of Scripture, without any addition or supply by way of interpretation" are we necessarily bound to accept. For in "places of ambiguous and doubtful or dark and intricate meaning it is sufficient if we religiously admire, acknowledge and confess; using that moderation of St Austin, not seeking to support or overturn either

[1] Hales, *Works*, vol. II: "Of dealing with Erring Christians."

opinion but only restraining ourselves from presumptuous confidence in our own judgments".[1]

Heresy and schism, again, "as they are in common use, are two theological scarecrows which they who uphold a party in religion use to fright away such, as making enquiry into it, are ready to relinquish and oppose it, if it appear either erroneous or suspicious". It is true that in some cases "dissension and disunion are often necessary", but then "not he that separates, but he that causes the separation is the schismatic". Where, however, the cause of schism is unnecessary (and of whether it is or is not necessary the individual *animo defoecato* must, as we have seen, be the judge) then both parties are schismatics equally. But Hales maintains that in cases of schism over matters of fact and over matters of opinion there has never been any real reason why the parties to the dispute should proceed so far as to disrupt the union of the Church. And here he openly rebukes both the Separatists and Laud for their unreasonable and uncharitable behaviour. Citing the Donatist schism as a schism over matter of fact, Hales asks why, even though the Donatists were in error, "it might not be lawful to go to Church with the Donatist, or to celebrate Easter with the Quarto-deciman, if occasion so require?...Nay what if those to whose care the execution of the public service is committed, do something either unseemly or suspicious, or peradventure unlawful? What if the garments they wear be censured, nay, indeed, be superstitious? What if the gesture of adoration be used at the altar, as now we have

[1] Hales, *Works*, vol. II: "Abuses of Hard Places in Scripture."

learned to speak? What if the homilist or preacher deliver any doctrine of the truth of which we are not well persuaded (a thing which very often falls out) yet for all this we may not separate unless we be constrained personally to bear a part in them ourselves." Hales, therefore, cannot see why "men of different opinions in Christian religion, may not hold communion in sacris and both go to one Church. Why may I not go, if occasion require, to an Arian Church, so there be no Arianism expressed in their liturgy? And were liturgies and public forms of service"—here Hales rebukes Laud as he had just done the Separatist—"so framed as they admitted not of particular and private fancies, but contained only such things, as in which all Christians do agree, schisms on opinions were utterly vanished.... If the spiritual guides and fathers of the Church would be a little sparing of encumbering churches with superfluities, and not over rigid either in reviving obsolete customs, or imposing new, there were far less danger of schism and superstition, and all the inconveniences likely to ensue would be but this, they should in so doing yield a little to the imbecillities of inferiors, a thing which St Paul would never have refused to do." It is thus that Hales' plea for reasonable and charitable behaviour leads him to a broad church policy of the latitudinarian.[1]

[1] Hales, *Works*, vol. i: "A Tract concerning Schism and Schismatics." This work was probably written for the benefit of Chillingworth in the controversy which led up to the *Religion of Protestants* (*vide infra*). The tract was not published until 1642.

Hales also suggests the ambition of bishops who set themselves up as *jure divino* as a third cause of schism. But Hales maintained episcopacy was merely an institution of human convenience. For

The use of violence in spiritual matters Hales deplores. The peace of the Church has often been destroyed by Christians who have sought to spread the gospel of Christ by the use of the arm of the flesh, and so have come to bloody persecutions. Against this confusion of powers Hales cites the testimony of St Hilary, who contrasts the experiences of Christ and the disciples, who spread the word by preaching only and were themselves persecuted, with that of later bishops, by whom violence is employed sometimes against true professors.[1] There is "great dissimilitude and unlikeness" between Christ's kingdom and the kingdoms of this world. For whereas in temporal kingdoms "nothing so usual as the sword and war: no kingdom of the world but by the sword is either gotten, or held or both", Christ's kingdom "is erected and maintained, not by the sword, but by the spirit; not by violence, but by love; not by striving, but by yielding, not by fighting, but by dying". In subjects, laws and location these two kingdoms differ: in subjects, because "everyone of us bears a double person". "This earth, that is, this body of clay, hath God given to the sons of men, to the princes under whose government we live; but heaven, that is, the inward and spiritual man, hath he reserved unto himself." Princes, therefore, "can restrain the outward man and moderate our outward actions, by edicts and laws they can tie our hands and our tongue;

the whole of this tract Hales was rebuked by Laud, but though, in his letter to the Archbishop, he made a personal submission, Hales made no real concessions in principle.

[1] Hales, *Works*, vol. III: "Peace the Legacy of Christ."

thus far they can go", but no farther, for "to set up an imperial throne in our understandings and wills, that part of our government belongs to God and Christ". Yet inasmuch as "inward government hath influence upon our outward actions, the authority of Kings over our outward man is not so absolute, but that it suffers a great restraint; it must stretch no farther than the prince of our inward man pleases: for if secular princes stretch out the skirts of their authority to command aught by which our souls are prejudiced, the King of souls hath given us in this case a greater command, 'That we obey God rather than man'." That "Christ's kingdom is not of this world" is therefore an effectual text for opening the nature of the Church. "For I know no error so common, so frequent, so hardly to be rooted out, so much hindering the knowledge of the true nature of the Church, as this that men do take the Church to be like unto the world." In recent times alone there have thence risen unnecessary emphasis upon the visibility of the Church;[1] exaggerated estimation of the importance of outward state and ceremony in the service of God, and unnecessary fears for persecuted Christians (for fire and sword cannot work desolation on the kingdom of God).[2]

It is, however, important to observe that in the sermon from which these quotations are taken Hales is

[1] This had arisen in disputes between Anglicans and Roman Catholics. The Catholics invariably asked where was the true church before Luther, unless it was the Roman Church? To which the Anglican replied that it was not necessary for a visible church to have persisted from early times, provided there was a continuity in the elect (who were indiscernible to men's eyes). *Vide* Chillingworth controversy.

[2] Hales, *Works*, vol. II: "Christ's Kingdom not of this world."

concerned with distinguishing between Christ's kingdom and the world, and that his reference to the Church
is only incidental. In other words it would be wrong to
assume that Hales is envisaging anything like the strict
separation of Church and State. He is merely doing
what we have remarked that all tolerationists of whatever
sort must do in practice: asserting his disbelief in the use
of force in certain spheres of human conduct, and therefore denying an ethical purpose to the sole authority
which in practice controls the use of force—the civil
power.[1] Moreover, that Hales in the last resort does not
deny coercive power to the Church is clear from his
sermon, *Of dealing with erring Christians*. The whole of
this sermon is an eloquent plea for the Church to exercise tolerance with those who in any way are in error,
and for that reasonable and charitable behaviour which
we have already noticed. Even the most seriously in
error—sect-makers, and those who have an heretical or
erring faith—should be treated with all tolerance, for
the Church should not seek to establish unity of opinion
so much as to provide that multiplicity of conceit
trouble not the Church's peace. Thereupon Hales
considers the history of the Church's treatment of
heretics. The Church never even excommunicated
heretics at first, but only used the buckler, and when she
took the sword into her hands, "some of her best and
chiefest captains much misliked it". It is true that the
Church did come to believe that there was more mercy
in punishing than forbearing. St Augustine retracted, as
the result of experience, his earlier injunction to deal

[1] *Vide* chap. I.

kindly with heretics. "Yet could I wish that it might be said of the Church which was sometimes observed of Augustus, 'He had been angry with and severely punished many of his kin, but he could never endure to cut off any of them by death'. But this I must request you to take only as my private wish and not as a censure, if anything have been done to the contrary" (a precaution against Laud). As David mourned Absalom, not as his heir, but because he was cut off in his sins, so the Church must be gentle to the sons that rise against her "loath to unsheath either sword, but most of all the temporal: for this were to send them quick despatch to hell". Now the permission to the Church to use coercive measures, which is implied, and not denied here, rather than explicitly asserted, might be accounted for on the grounds of Hales' natural caution against Laud with whom he had already once had a (not unfriendly) controversy. Hales' real opinions are clearly on the side of complete tolerance. But he does go on to describe English policy towards the Papists as a "perfect pattern for dealing with erring Christians". The statutes against the Papists are only such as to cause them to consider the innocency of the Church they refuse; priests sent into England are either sent back, or suffer an easy restraint to prevent them spreading poisonous opinions; and only for treasonable practices is blood shed. The use of civil force against the Papists for their opinions is justified on other than wholly political grounds here. The argument that civil force is used only to cause the Papist to reconsider his views is precisely the position that Locke demolished in his *Letters on Toleration*. It is

156

the last line of defence of those who, admitting that men cannot be forced into salvation, yet wish to defend the use of civil force in religious affairs.

It is in this same sermon, too, that, considering those who, because they are weak in faith, ought not to be received to doubtful disputations, Hales protests against "this promiscuous and careless admission to the hearing and handling of controversies" which was an especial vice of his age. "For disputation, though it be an excellent help for bringing the truth to light, yet many times, by too much troubling the waters, it suffers it to slip away unseen, especially when the meaner sort are concerned, who cannot so easily espy when it is mixed with sophistry and deceit." Hales adopted this position precisely because he did not believe (as John Stuart Mill did) that truth was attainable solely by the use of reason, but believed that it must be "illuminated by revelation out of God's word". However much, therefore, Hales might maintain that it "is a thing very profitable that divers tracts be written, by divers men, after divers fashions", it must always be "according to the same analogy of faith". The fundamentals to salvation to him, although few, yet remained necessary fundamentals. But although this is an undoubted restriction on absolute liberty of thought, there is much wisdom in Hales' complaint against those who "fill the Lord's floor with chaff" (for the question of truth and error, the wheat and the tares, is not here involved). A religious Justinian, making theological Pandects, would enable "infinite store of books peaceably to be buried, and after ages reap greater profit with smaller cost and pains".[1] With these sentiments the greater minds of the early seventeenth century were, as we shall see, in complete agreement.[2]

Hales' conception of toleration, although, in the main, the product of his own reasonableness and spiritual individualism,[3] was formed under the influence of both the Arminian and Socinian movements. The letters from the Synod of Dort which Hales wrote to Sir Dudley Carlton, English ambassador at the Hague, reveal a marked movement from original and undisguised hostility towards the Arminian Remonstrants, to a much more sympathetic consideration of their views, though to the end of the Synod Hales supported (in spirit) the Counter-Remonstrants. There is no doubt that his experiences at the Synod had a profound effect upon Hales. Not only did it lead him to "say goodnight to John Calvin", but the dogmatism there exhibited led him to question the whole value of theological dogma.[4] And the great plea of Episcopius for toleration so impressed him, that in the later works which we have examined Hales used many of the arguments that Episcopius had employed on that occasion.[5] It is, however, important to appreciate that, in England, the

---

[1] Hales, *Works*, vol. II: "Of dealing with erring Christians."

[2] Especially, of course, Robert Burton in *The Anatomy of Melancholy*.

[3] It has been seen how unimportant Hales considered outward state and ceremony in the service of God. In the sermon "Abuses of Hard Places in Scripture" he further suggests that we are not even bound to accept the literal meaning of Scripture if the Holy Ghost treads out another way.   [4] Tulloch, *op. cit.* I, 191.

[5] The Letters from the Synod of Dort are in Hales, *Works*, vol. III.

influence of Arminianism was very far from being always on the side of religious liberty. Dogmatically the Arminian movement in England became allied with the Laudian High Church movement,[1] and, as Selden acutely observed, "the Puritans, who will allow no free will at all, but God does all, yet will allow the subject his liberty to do, or not to do, notwithstanding the King, the God upon earth. The Arminians, who hold we have free will, yet say, when we come to the King, there must be all obedience, and no liberty to be stood for."[2] The political theory of the Dutch Arminians sought toleration by means of the intervention of the civil power in religious disputes,[3] but this permission to the civil power of jurisdiction in religious causes might well be employed to defend the peace of the Church by other methods than those of toleration—by suppressing factious sectaries, for example. The possibility of the State using its power in religious causes for other ends than that of promoting general tolerance is always a danger which accompanies the political system and theory of the latitudinarian tolerationist.

His "Confession of the Trinity"[4] is sufficient to dispel the charges of Socinianism made against Hales,[5] but

[1] Tulloch, *op. cit.* I, 72. [2] Selden, J., *Table Talk*, "Freewill".
[3] *Vide* chap. II. [4] Hales, *Works*, I, 76
[5] Aubrey, for example, writing long after Hales' death, still persists in describing him as "the first Socinian in England". Aubrey's testimony is unreliable not only because of his love of idle gossip, but also because he makes the same remark about several other people. Nevertheless, Aubrey may have meant no more than "rational theologian" by Socinian, because it was for their rationalism that the Socinians were most disliked, and in this case the aptness of his remark is obvious.

there can be little doubt that he was influenced by the rational theology of the Socinian movement. This is clear, not only from the injunction of Suckling to "leave Socinus and the schoolmen" at Eton, but from two pamphlets by two Polish Socinians which were published in Latin in 1628 and 1633 in England, and which were at first widely attributed to Hales.[1] In style and method these two pamphlets are wholly unlike the work of Hales, but there is a marked affinity of thought. The first of these pamphlets, the *Dissertatio de Pace et Concordia Ecclesiae* by Samuel Przipcovius (which, in Holland, was attributed to Episcopius, as, in England, it was to Hales), was an explicit and rational plea for toleration in the Church. After observing how "we are more enamoured of our errors than of all our darlings, either because they wink at the scapes and dalliances of our affections, or because we are enraged against dissenters with obstinate prejudice and frantic affectation of parties", the author condemns the practice of seeking eternal salvation by mere confessions of faith instead of by holiness of life, whereby the least error in faith is reckoned as a greater sin than the foulest of crimes. This blind and precipitant condemning of others proceeds from rashness of defining, and the assumption of infallible judgment.[2] For where, indeed, is truth to be found amongst so many hundreds of sects? If a man amongst so many has not chosen the true it is absurd to reproach his honesty with an inevitable failure of his

[1] For an account of the history of this misconception *vide* P. des Maizeaux, *An historical and critical account of the life and writings of the ever memorable Mr John Hales*, p. 5, note.

[2] *Dissertatio de Pace*, chap. I (in *The Phoenix Tracts*, vol. II).

understanding.[1] As, therefore, the things necessary to salvation are but few, and consist in holiness of life rather than confessions of faith, in simple obedience to God rather than abstruse theologies,[2] so even "heretics" should be tolerated in the Church so long as they do nothing impious to God, and testify their love for the Lord Jesus by obeying His commandments.[3] In the time of the Apostles, heresy necessarily involved manifest depravity, since to resist the opinion of the Apostles was to resist the infallible word of God. But now there is no such infallible judge, and therefore those that err, even in matters of great weight, must be tolerated in the Church, provided they deny not Christ.[4] "Voluntary rebels against the divine majesty" do, indeed, exist (such as manifest patrons of vice, and anyone denying the resurrection of the dead); and these, as they bring unto the Church doctrines tending to subvert salvation and faith, may legitimately be excommunicated. "But those doctrines that stand not within the boundaries of necessity to salvation are such that an error in them, especially in this disturbed state of things, cannot be taxed of wilful pravity, nor can it either damn its author, or exclude him from the bosom of the Church." The primitive Church could suffer, in her strength and vigour, such violent operations (as excommunication) which the Church of to-day, with little young blood in her veins, could not possibly stand. "Believe me, yet that talk of nothing but lancets and cauteries, will with your unseasonable physic kill the Church, if ye let out

---

[1] *Ibid*. chap. XI.
[2] *Ibid*. chaps. II–VII.
[3] *Ibid*. chap. XI.
[4] *Ibid*. chap. XII.

that little blood which is remaining in this nick of time when she seems to be almost a-dying."[1] This pamphlet is remarkable, therefore, in regarding even the ex-communication of those in error as a form of persecution, and not merely the use of civil force against them, being excommunicated, by the State. For the author believes that, were a state of mutual toleration established, truth would of itself overcome error "inasmuch as the nature of truth is such that, like to eagles feathers, she devours all other light plumage of opinions". To refuse a tolera-tion is the clearest indication that a sect has no faith in the truth of its cause.[2]

The second pamphlet, the *Brevis Disquisitio* by Joachimus Stegmannus, whom des Maizeaux describes as a "celebrated Socinian minister",[3] was an attempt to indicate to the Protestants that their logical strength in refuting the attacks of the Papists would be increased if they adopted certain Socinian principles, and depended less on the Papists' own grounds.[4] Thus, in attempting to decide the judge of controversies of faith, which the Papists declared to be of necessity an infallible Pope, the Protestants weakened their position by admitting the authority of Fathers and Doctors. The true judge is right

---

[1] *Dissertatio de Pace*, chap. XII.

[2] *Ibid.* chap. XI. Three chapters of this work (VIII–X) are also devoted to a brief apologia for Socinianism—how it excludes none but patrons of vice from salvation, is based entirely on Scripture and not on human traditions, etc.

[3] The *Brevis Disquisitio* is also in *The Phoenix Tracts*, vol. II.

[4] The first half of the seventeenth century in England witnessed much theological debate between Catholics and Anglicans. *Vide* the ensuing consideration of the Chillingworth controversy, and also chap. VIII.

reason, for "by the judgment of right reason it is discovered what everyone meaneth, of what force his testimony is, and how much it recedeth from truth and falsehood". God gave us reason to understand, and to judge, as He gave us the eye to see. It is foolish to say that reason can bring no certainty. For if philosophy can agree on the principles of geometry, likewise in divine things there will be agreement enough, and, for the rest, doubting is often the cause of study and wisdom.[1] Similarly, in determining the rule of controversies, Protestants weaken their position, first, by in practice admitting the authority of tradition, and secondly, by rejecting the principles of natural reason in making Scripture theoretically the sole rule. The true rule of controversies of faith is Scripture, interpreted where necessary by philosophical principles.[2] After a consideration of certain particular errors of Protestants that weaken them against the Papists,[3] the pamphlet concludes with a plea for mutual toleration. For as truth is the strongest of all weapons with which to oppose error, so violence is a weakness when employed by any religion, not merely when used by the Papists, for "how can ye blame the Papists for that which you indulge in yourselves?" All men believe they have the truth. Now if Protestants hold they cannot err, why should they not allow that the Papists also cannot? But if they hold that they can, "why suffer they not those that dissent, why do they not hear them, why do they prohibit their books to be read and sold?"[4] Specifically Socinian doctrines

[1] *Brevis Disquisitio*, chaps. I–IV.
[2] *Ibid*. chaps. V–VII.
[3] *Ibid*. chaps. VIII–XI.
[4] *Ibid*. chap. XII.

11-2

are introduced into this pamphlet only incidentally and covertly.[1] The pamphlet has less affinity to the works of Hales (who, save for the *Tract on Schism*, which was written privately for Chillingworth's benefit, concerned himself little with the English dispute between Protestants and Catholics) than to those of William Chillingworth, who was not only the greatest Protestant apologist in England in the early seventeenth century, but was also the first Anglican in the dispute with Rome really to adopt the principles which this pamphlet had advocated.[2]

II
WILLIAM CHILLINGWORTH

The Religion of Protestants a safe way to Salvation by William Chillingworth was by far the most distinguished work produced in a long controversy between Anglicans and Roman Catholics which extended from 1630 to 1652. In 1630 a Roman Catholic who had taken the name of Edward Knott, but whose real name was Matthew Wilson, published a work entitled *Charity Mistaken, with the want whereof Catholics are unjustly charged: for affirming, as ˙they do with grief, that Protestantcy unrepented destroys Salvation.* A reply to this was published in 1633 by Dr Christopher Potter entitled *Want of Charity justly charged*, and which was not without some of the liberal ideas which were later to find a complete expression in *The Religion of Protestants*.

[1] Wood, A., *Athen. Oxon.*, Hales.
[2] Both the *Dissertatio de Pace* and the *Brevis Disquisitio* were published in English in 1653 and when they were reprinted in *The Phoenix Tracts* they were still attributed (though doubtfully) to Hales.

Rejecting the claim to infallibility of both the Pope and General Councils,[1] Potter emphasized that the unity of the Church consists in unity of faith which will tolerate and compound differences, and not in unity of opinions, and that although there should be no dissension over the fundamentals to salvation, yet in things secondary and accidental dissension is a profitable means of finding truth. "As in a musical consort, a discord now and then (so it be in the descant and depart not from the ground) sweetens the harmony; so the variety of opinions, or of rites in parts of the Church doth rather commend than prejudice the unity of the whole."[2] And all the fundamental beliefs necessary to salvation are contained in the Apostles' Creed.[3] To Dr Potter Knott replied in 1634 in *Mercy and Truth, or Charity maintained by Catholics*, which was designed "to show that amongst men of different religions, one side can only be saved. For since there must be some infallible means to decide all controversies concerning religion, and to propound truths revealed by Almighty God; and this means can be no other but the visible Church of Christ, which at the time of Luther's appearance was only the Church of Rome, and such as agreed with her; we must conclude that whoever opposeth himself to her definitions, or forsaketh her communion, doth resist God himself, whose spouse she is, and whose divine truth she propounds; and therefore becomes guilty of schism and heresy, which, since Luther his associates and Protestants have done, and still continue to do, it is not want

[1] Potter, C., *Want of Charity justly charged*, sect. 5.
[2] *Ibid.* sect. 2.   [3] *Ibid.* sect. 7.

of charity, but abundance of evident cause, that forceth us to declare this necessary truth: Protestantcy unrepented destroys salvation."[1] Hearing that Chillingworth was preparing a reply to this work, Knott further issued in 1636 *A direction to be observed by N. N.*, in which, in advance of the publication of *The Religion of Protestants*, he accused Chillingworth of Socinianism, of reducing all Christian faith to natural reason.[2]

The Religion of Protestants was published in 1638 as a reply to *Charity Maintained*. It is a long, systematic, though immensely involved, work containing much liberal thinking and able writing. According to the practice of his age, Chillingworth replied sentence by sentence to Knott, and when it is remembered that *Charity Maintained* was itself an answer to an answer, it will be appreciated how complex the structure of *The Religion of Protestants* is. The question at issue between Chillingworth and Knott is not necessarily relevant to the problem of toleration. The works of Knott which we have so far examined contained no explicit statement of a theory of persecution, nor does the belief in exclusive salvation necessarily involve the conviction that men may be forced to it (the English Baptists believed that

---

[1] Knott, E., *Charity Maintained*, chap. VII.
[2] Chapter II of *A Direction to be observed by N. N.* contains, incidentally, interesting confirmation of the thesis of Mr Basil Willey in *The Seventeenth-Century Background*. In examining the reasons why so many embrace Socinianism (which Knott himself identifies with "reducing all Christian faith to natural reason"), Knott suggests, amongst other things, that it is due to the Protestant abandonment of the Scholastic Philosophy which leaves them with no systematic philosophic reply to the Socinians, who base all upon reason.

far fewer men would be saved than did Laud). But Chillingworth made the problem of toleration relevant incidentally, and therefore we shall examine *The Religion of Protestants*, not from the point of view of Chillingworth's reply to Knott, but from that of the problems whence we have seen the idea of toleration arise. It is, however, important to appreciate this context in which they are set.

Like Hales, of whom he was a friend and fellow member of Lord Falkland's circle at Great Tew, Chillingworth devoted his life to the pursuit of truth. "My Lord Falkland and he", writes Aubrey, "had such extraordinarily clear reasons, that they were wont to say at Oxon that if the Great Turk were to be converted by natural reason, these two were the persons to convert him." It was at Oxford that Chillingworth, attracted by the logical strength of the absolute and infallible claims of the Roman Church, was converted to Roman Catholicism by the Jesuit Fisher, who had held the conference with Laud before the Countess of Buckingham. A short period at Douai, however, convinced Chillingworth of his mistake, though not before he had published the reasons for his conversion to which he was afterwards to write an answer. Reflecting on this period of indecision in his life in *The Religion of Protestants* Chillingworth recounted how he saw, and still sees, "that there are Popes against Popes, Councils against Councils, some Fathers against others, the same Fathers against themselves, a consent of Fathers of one age against the consent of Fathers of another age, the Church of one age against the Church of another age.

Traditive interpretations of Scripture are pretended; but there are few or none to be found."[1] But when he wrote this Chillingworth had arrived at the truth which it was the main business of his life to propagate, and which, in some sense, is his main thesis in *The Religion of Protestants*. As "the Bible only is the religion of Protestants", so this Scripture contains within it all things necessary to salvation.[2] For various circumstances Chillingworth holds it impossible to give a precise catalogue of fundamentals,[3] but "the sum of his whole direction" to any man seeking salvation is this. "Believe the Scripture to be the word of God, use your true endeavour to find the true sense of it, and live according to it, and then you may rest securely you are in the true way of eternal happiness."[4]

It follows, therefore, that, for his age, Chillingworth conceived a very broad way to salvation, and he insists that it is not the form of the Gospels that matters so much as the substance of them. For "if a man should believe Christian religion wholly and entirely, and live according to it, such a man, though he should not know or not believe the Scripture to be a rule of faith, no, nor to be the word of God, my opinion is he may be saved".[5] Moreover "God hath not so clearly and plainly declared himself... but that an honest man, whose heart is right to God, and one that is a true lover of God and of his truth, may, by reason of the conflict of contrary reasons

[1] Chillingworth, W., *Religion of Protestants*, Answer to chap. 6. 56.
[2] *Ibid*.
[3] *Ibid*. Answer to chap. 3. 13.
[4] *Ibid*. Answer to chap. 4. 53.
[5] *Ibid*. Answer to chap. 2. 159. *Vide* also *ibid*. 89.

on both sides, very easily, and therefore excusably, mistake and embrace error for truth; and reject truth for error". If any Protestant or Papist is betrayed into such error, or kept in any error by any sin of his will, though the error is in itself damnable, yet it is not "exclusive of all hope of salvation, but pardonable, if discovered, upon a particular, explicit repentance; if not discovered, upon a general and implicit repentance for all sins known and unknown; in which number all sinful errors must of necessity be contained".[1] "Nothing is necessary to be believed but what is plainly revealed. For to say, that when a place of Scripture, by reason of ambiguous terms lies indifferent between divers senses, whereof one is true and the other is false, that God obliges men under pain of damnation not to mistake through error and human frailty is to make God a tyrant; and to say that he requires us certainly to attain that end, for the attaining whereof we have no certain means is to say that like Pharaoh he gives no straw, and requires brick; that he reaps where he sows not; that he gathers where he strews not, that he will not be pleased with our utmost endeavours to please him without full, exact, and never failing performance."[2] Moreover even though "Scripture, reason and authority were all on one side, and the appearances of the other side all easily answerable; yet if we consider the strange power that education and prejudices instilled by it, have over even excellent

---

[1] *Ibid.* Answer to Preface, 26. Chillingworth thus admits Papists to salvation on precisely the same conditions as any others he believes to be in error. *Vide* also Answer to chap. 3. 12.

[2] *Ibid.* Answer to chap. 2. 104.

understandings, we may well imagine that many truths which in themselves are revealed plainly enough, are yet to such or such a man, prepossessed with contrary opinions, not revealed plainly. Neither doubt I but God who knows whereof we are made, and what passions we are subject unto, will compassionate such infirmities, and not enter into judgment with us for those things, which, all things considered, were unavoidable."[1] Chillingworth also indicates that in cases of necessity— as, for example, in that of a Christian living alone amongst Pagans—the ministrations of the Church can be safely dispensed with.[2]

The application which Chillingworth makes of this doctrinal liberalism to the more practical problems of schism and heresy, whence persecution proceeds, is often repeated in the course of *The Religion of Protestants*, for the simplicity of Chillingworth's counsel did not prevent him from realizing how to many it is difficult to follow, and therefore how, in practice, it is frequently ignored. Replying to the argument of Knott that the Church must be universally infallible, for otherwise unity of faith could not be conserved against every wind of doctrine, Chillingworth points out how Roman Catholics are, because of this, unable to appreciate "that there can be any means to conserve the unity of the faith, but only that which conserves their authority over the faithful" (and which, of course, implies a theory of theological persecution). But if all men are left to their liberty, provided they improve it not to a

[1] Chillingworth, W., *Religion of Protestants*, Answer to chap. 3. 19.
[2] *Ibid*. Answer to chap. 5. 17.

tyranny over others, Scripture will be found infallible enough to compass this end. "And if it fail hereof, the reason is not any insufficiency or invalidity in the means, but the voluntary perverseness of the subjects it has to deal with: who, if they would be themselves, and be content that others should be, in the choice of their religions, the servants of God and not of men; if they would allow that the way to heaven is not narrower now than Christ left it; that the belief of no more difficulties is required now to salvation, than was in the Primitive Church; that no error is in itself destructive and exclusive from salvation now, that was not then; if instead of being zealous Papists, earnest Calvinists, rigid Lutherans, they would become themselves and be content that others should be plain and honest Christians; if all men would believe the Scripture, and freeing themselves from prejudice and passion, would sincerely endeavour to find the true sense of it, and live according to it, and require no more of others but to do so; nor denying their communion to any that do so, would so order their public service of God, that all which do so may without scruple, or hypocrisy, or protestation against any part of it, join with them in it: who doth not see that seeing all necessary truths are plainly and evidently set down in Scripture there would be of necessity among all men, in all things necessary unity of opinion? And notwithstanding any other differences that are or could be, unity of communion, and charity and mutual toleration? By which means all schism and heresy would be banished the world, and those wretched contentions that now rend and tear in pieces not the coat, but the members and bowels of Christ, which mutual pride and tyranny, and cursing, and killing and damning would fain make immortal, should speedily receive a most blessed catastrophe."[1] Here the rejection of a narrow, exclusive salvation, and the belief in reasonable and charitable behaviour, leads Chillingworth, as it had led Hales, to a broad Church policy, to the attainment of such unity as is essential by the methods of liberty rather than authority. Roman Catholics maintain "you must not use your own reason, nor your judgment, but refer all to the Church and believe her to be conformable to antiquity. ...For my part I am certain that God hath given us our reason to discern between truth and falsehood, and he that makes not this use of it, but believes things he knows not why; I say, it is by chance he believes the truth and not by choice; and I cannot but fear that God will not accept of this 'sacrifice of fools'."[2] Nor is this to refer the choice between truth and falsehood to mere "private spirit", for reason is "a public and certain thing, exposed to all men's trial and examination",[3] the "gift of God, given to direct us in all our actions, in the use of Scripture".[4] For Chillingworth, Christians can be reduced to unity of communion, not "by taking away the diversity of opinions touching matters of religion", but by "showing that the diversity of opinions which is among the several sects of Christians, ought to be no hindrance to their unity in communion". "Christians

[1] Chillingworth, W., *Religion of Protestants*, Answer to chap. 3. 81.
[2] *Ibid*. Answer to chap. 2. 113.
[3] *Ibid*. Answer to chap. 2. 110.
[4] *Ibid*. Answer to chap. 6. 55.

must be taught to set a higher value upon those high points of faith and obedience wherein they agree, than upon those matters of less moment wherein they differ."[1] Chillingworth thus believed that the solution of the problems of a divided and persecuting Christendom lay with each individual, rather than in the mechanical separation of Church and State. For such advice as we have seen him give "cannot but be very fit to end all controversies necessary to be ended. For others that are not so, they will end when the world ends, and that is time enough".[2]

Nevertheless, on occasions, Chillingworth does express his views on the more specific problems of toleration and persecution. He appreciates, for example, that as Church and State have different ends, so the means which are adopted to settle civil disputes cannot be applied in controversies of faith. In civil disputes a judge is necessary not only to supplement human law by natural reason, but in some cases to moderate its rigour. The sentence of a civil judge must be enforced on both parties to the dispute by the civil power, for although they always remain free to think the sentence wrong, and, if they should desire, so to proclaim it,[3] it yet remains a duty to submit to the judge's decision. But in controversies of faith there is neither room nor need for such a judge, not only because a judge is necessarily a party to any religious dispute, but because Scripture is a perfect rule of faith, and needs neither

[1] *Ibid*. Answer to chap. 4. 39, 40.
[2] *Ibid*. Answer to chap. 2. 12.
[3] *Ibid*. Answer to chap. 2. 117.

supplement nor moderation. Whereas, too, in civil controversies both parties cannot be right, and the one usually damages the other, in "controversies of religion the case is otherwise. I may hold my opinion and do you no wrong, and you yours and do me none. Nay, we may both of us hold our opinion, and yet do ourselves no harm, provided the difference be not touching anything necessary to salvation." And if a civil judge is not necessary, still less is the power which he uses to enforce his decisions permissible. For in religious controversies it is essential to have a judge who adjudges right, for "all the power in the world is neither fit to convince, nor able to compel a man's conscience to consent to anything. Worldly terror may prevail so far as to make men profess a religion they believe not (such men, I mean, who know not there is a heaven provided for martyrs, and a hell for those that dissemble such truths as are necessary to be professed). But to force either any man to believe what he believes not, or any honest man to dissemble what he does believe, all the powers of the world are too weak, with all the powers in hell to assist them."[1] Further, in considering the parable of the wheat and the tares being left together till the harvest, which Knott had used, identifying "the field" with the Church, to show that corruption in manners yields no sufficient cause to leave the Church (which is precisely what the Protestants had done), Chillingworth identified "the field" with the world, and said that excommunication merely put men out of the Church into the world "where we

[1] Chillingworth, W., *Religion of Protestants*, Answer to chap. 2. 14-23.

174

may converse with them freely without scandal to the Church". Catholics, therefore, disobey the command, "Let them both grow up till the harvest", in rooting the tares (such as are heretics) out of the world, while Protestants do not disobey it by ejecting manifest heretics and notorious sinners out of the Church.[1] But, as with Hales, Chillingworth is arguing in both these instances, not the legal separation of Church and State, but the necessity for denying, in some degree, an ethical purpose to force, without which no measure of toleration could be achieved.

How far, then, is Chillingworth prepared to deny the use of force in religious affairs? His appreciation of the evils which accompany the use of force in religious matters could not be more complete. "Human violence may make men counterfeit, but cannot make them believe, and is therefore fit for nothing, but to breed form without and atheism within. Besides if this means of bringing men to embrace any religion were generally used (as if it may justly be used in any place by those that have power, and think they have truth, certainly they cannot with reason deny but that it may be used in every place, by those that have power as well as they, and think they have truth as well as they). What would follow but the maintenance perhaps of truth, but perhaps only of the profession of it, in one place and the oppression of it in an hundred? What will follow from it but the preservation peradventure of unity, but peradventure only of uniformity, in particular States and Churches; but the immortalizing of greater and more

[1] *Ibid.* Answer to chap. 5. 57.

lamentable divisions of Christendom and the world? And therefore what can follow from it, but perhaps in the judgment of carnal policy, the temporal benefit and tranquillity of temporal states and kingdoms, but the infinite prejudice, if not the desolation of the kingdom of Christ?'' After asserting "that there is no danger to any state from any man's opinion", Chillingworth proceeds to give some exceptions, which constitute the cases in which he is prepared to allow civil force to be used in matter of religion or opinion. First, "an opinion by which disobedience to authority, or impiety is taught or licensed...may justly be punished as well as other faults". Secondly, there is a danger to the safety of the State from an opinion to which "this sanguinary doctrine is joined"—that it is lawful to force others to it by human violence.[1] Chillingworth does not explicitly assert that this second type of opinion should be suppressed, though that is perhaps the implication of the passage. Elsewhere Chillingworth adds that the civil judge "may proceed with certainty enough against all seditious persons, such as draw men to disobedience either against Church or State, as well as against rebels and traitors, and thieves and murderers".[2] Should the civil magistrate use a tyrannous violence, though it may be avoided by flight "yet may it not be resisted by opposing violence against it". Christians should choose rather to die for their religion than fight for it.[3]

Now it should be observed that all these permissions

[1] Chillingworth, W., *Religion of Protestants*, Answer to chap. 5.96.
[2] *Ibid*. Answer to chap. 2. 122.   [3] *Ibid*. Answer to chap. 5. 96.

of the use of civil power in religious matters are extremely vague, and might allow a greater or less interference by the State according to the interpretation placed upon them. If, for example, "impiety" means no more than "blasphemy" then his permission to punish it cannot be considered a very serious mitigation of religious liberty. Again permission to suppress an opinion which preaches the use of violence to force men to it, simply on the ground that it encourages the general use of violence, might well be approved by even a most devoted believer in religious liberty. For it is by no means easy to decide whether or not liberty may be partially sacrificed in the present (by the suppression of a sect threatening itself to suppress all liberty of thought on its accession to power) in order the more securely to preserve it in the future. To take a modern example, had it occurred, there would have been, at all events, a case to be made out, from the point of view of liberty of thought, in defence of the suppression of the National Socialist party in Germany before it came to a position of power, even had it then merely preached the suppression of other opinions by violence, and not also practised it. On the other hand it cannot be denied that Chillingworth's permission to punish all "seditious persons, such as draw men to disobedience either against Church or State" might well be used to justify the most extreme of persecutions. It is possible of course that Chillingworth might have liked to express himself more explicitly (for his book had to pass Laud's censors who would scarcely permit an open censure of the régime). But it is precisely the meaningless ambiguity of these phrases that Knott seized upon in the first of his replies to *The Religion of Protestants* which he entitled *Christianity Maintained*. This work was largely occupied in charging Chillingworth with Socinianism, with reducing all faith to reason, and thereby subverting Christianity. Its motive was to discredit Chillingworth with his ecclesiastical superiors. In reply to Chillingworth's policy of toleration, Knott urges not only that it will beget "unchristian errors and atheisms", but implies that Chillingworth intended thereby a censure of the policy of his superiors. As for the limitations to this toleration, Chillingworth's first limitation "either destroys all that he said before, or else it is but a verbal gloss for his own security. For if he grants that every heresy is impiety, and brings with it disobedience to authority (as certainly it does if it be professed against the laws of the Kingdom, or decrees and commands of the Church, State and Prelates where the contrary is maintained). If, I say, his meaning be this then his former general doctrine vanisheth into nothing, and it will remain true, that men may be punished for their opinions and heresies. But if his meaning be, that no opinion is to be punished except such as implies disobedience to authority, or licenseth impiety in things which merely belong to temporal affairs, and concern only the civil comportment of men one to another, as theft, murder and the like, then he still leaves a freedom for men to believe and profess what they please in matter of religion." Thereby the policy of the English prelates is openly censured, and, under the second limitation, it is implied that they may even be punished, since the prelates themselves teach the right to enforce contrary believers.[1]

In *The Church Conquerant over human wit*, another reply to *The Religion of Protestants*, John Floyd further indicated the logical consequence of Chillingworth's views on toleration. If Chillingworth justifies the Protestant separation from the Roman Church on the ground that, if a man believe a religion to be consonant to Scripture, and therefore true, he must, if the situation demands it, forsake the Church he holds to be erroneous; then he must likewise permit the further separation of "Puritans, Brownists, Anabaptists, Arians, Socinians and Tritheists who know that to them the Church of England seemeth false".[2] This is a practical illustration of what Chillingworth had been content to maintain in general, theoretical, terms.

But despite these uncertainties as to the exact extent of the practical religious liberty that Chillingworth was prepared to allow, there can be no doubt that, as with Hales, the whole weight of his influence was lent to the cause of tolerance. And although in both cases the religious liberty which they envisage is less explicit, and possibly less secure, than that which the Baptists envisaged when they separated Church and State, their approach to the whole question is in many ways more fundamental. For however much may be done to secure liberty by political devices, its security rests always

[1] Knott, E., *Christianity Maintained*, chap. XI.
[2] Floyd, J., *The Church Conquerant over human wit*, chap. VI. There were several other replies to *The Religion of Protestants*. The last—*Infidelity Unmasked*, by E. Knott—was not published until 1652, nine years after Chillingworth's death.

12-2

upon the reasonableness of the individuals by whom and to whom it is granted. Toleration is, after all, a personal human problem as well as a social and a political, and one cannot expect the State to be tolerant if the individuals who compose it are not first tolerant themselves. In addressing themselves, therefore, to the individual, both Hales and Chillingworth were offering a broader and more permanent solution to the problem of persecution than could be achieved by any oaths of allegiance, or mechanical separation of Church and State, important, for the moment, as these may be. And if their approach was more fundamental, their observations were historically more influential than the works of the English Baptists (though, of course, this of itself is no virtue in either). Both Hales and Chillingworth were Royalists, Anglicans and friends of Archbishop Laud,[1] and the birth of the idea of toleration in the governing body of the Anglican Church cannot but be considered of greater significance for the practical achievement of toleration than the works of obscure and persecuted Separatists (though this is in no way to detract from the intrinsic theoretical merit of these works). On the immediate future the influence of Chillingworth and Hales was negligible (the kingdom of the saints could scarcely be expected to listen to the counsels of reason), but after the Restoration, and even during the Civil War, there were not wanting many to continue and develop the line of thought of which Chillingworth and Hales had been such distinguished exponents.

[1] Especially Chillingworth, who was Laud's godson.

CHAPTER VII

THE THEORY OF THE LAY
LATITUDINARIANS

IN the present chapter the theory of some distinguished laymen will be considered. In some cases
their thought was little more than an approximation
to the idea of religious liberty, and there are considerable
divergences amongst them over the persons to whom it
should be applied. But in the nature of their thought,
and in their common latitudinarian approach to the
problems of persecution and a divided Christendom
Francis Bacon, Robert Burton, John Selden, Sir Thomas
Browne and Lord Herbert of Cherbury exhibit a marked
affinity to each other, and to the views of the more
specifically Anglican latitudinarians which have just
been considered. They may, therefore, be said to
represent the reaction of early seventeenth-century
problems upon men of the greatest intellectual ability,
to whom theology was but one of the many branches of
thought.

John Earle in *Micro-Cosmographie* characterized a
"sceptic in religion" as one who, amongst other things,
"is troubled at the naturalness of religion to countries,
that Protestantism should be born so in England and
Popery abroad, and that fortune and the stars should so
much share in it". "He cannot think so many wise men
should be in error, and so many honest men out of the

way, and his wonder is doubled when he sees these oppose one another." This distress at the diversity of truth, and the consequent desire to replace it by a new philosophic synthesis, is especially characteristic of Bacon and of Herbert in his *De Veritate*. "J'avoue que le combat et la contradiction des opinions m'ont bien donné de la peine, considérant que les uns estiment leurs doctrines véritables, et appellent les autres faussaires, menteurs et imposteurs et que ceux-ci en disent autant d'eux: de sorte que je n'ai pas trouvé aucun lieu pour reposer mon esprit, comme étant requis de renoncer à mes propres facultés, et d'embrasser celles des autres: et finalement l'on me commande de quitter ma propre raison ou l'on ne me menace de rien que de la damnation éternelle (suivant quelques doctrines) si je résiste tant soit peu."[1] As a purely personal problem these facts are less distressing to Browne in *Religio Medici*, to Burton in *The Anatomy of Melancholy* and to Selden in his *Table Talk*. Browne is quietly confident of the sufficiency for his own life of his own views and prejudices, and Burton takes an almost Rabelaisian delight in the infinite variety and diversity of human beliefs and follies, while Selden has too much cynical worldly wisdom to perturb himself at a cleric's damnation. But as an intellectual and political problem these facts were unescapable, because it was from the divisions of Christendom that there proceeded recriminatory persecutions, and threats to the security of Church and State as well as to the individuals of whom they were composed.

[1] Lord Herbert, *De Veritate*, p. 4 of French edit. of 1639.

It follows, therefore, that all these writers were quick
to reject, in varying degrees, the doctrine of a narrow
and exclusive salvation, and to deplore the insistence of
many divines upon certain things as fundamental which
ought not to be so considered. It is true that Bacon
insists that as God "is a jealous God his worship and
religion will endure no mixture and partner"; but,
considering the bounds of such necessary unity, he also
insists that men should distinguish "points fundamental
and of substance in religion" from "points not merely
of faith, but of opinion, order or good intention".[1]
Selden protests against Bancroft's insistence upon sub-
scription to the "King's supremacy, to the Common
Prayer, and to the Thirty-nine Articles" because "many
of them do not contain matter of faith. Is it matter of
faith how the Church should be governed? whether
infants should be baptized? whether we have any pro-
perty in our goods?"[2] Burton finds a symptom of
religious melancholy in that "we do aliud agere, are
zealous without knowledge, and too solicitous about that
which is not necessary, busying ourselves about im-
pertinent, needless, vain and idle ceremonies, populo ut
placerent, as the Jews did about sacrifices, oblations,
offerings, incense, new moons, feasts &c., but as Isaiah
taxeth them i. 12 who required this at your hands?"[3]
And later he attacks, with a superb confidence in the
truth of his own opinions, "all heretics and schismatics

[1] Bacon, *Essays*: "Of Unity in Religion."
[2] Selden, *Table Talk*: "Articles."
[3] Burton, *Anatomy of Melancholy*, part III, sect. IV, mem. I,
subs. I.

whatsoever", because "they do not only persecute and hate, but pity all other religions, account them damned, blind, as if they alone were the true Church, they are the true heirs, have the fee simple of heaven by a peculiar donation, 'tis entailed on them and their posterities, their doctrine sound, per funem aureum de caelo delapsa doctrina, they alone are to be saved."[1] Sir Thomas Browne refuses "to stand in diameter and swords points with" those who remain Roman Catholics, because "we have reformed from them, not against them for (omitting those improperations and terms of scurrility betwixt us, which only difference our affections, and not our cause) there is between us one common name and appellation, one faith and necessary body of principles common to us both". And although "I do desire with God that all, but yet affirm with men that few, shall know salvation; that the bridge is narrow, the passage strait unto life: yet those who do confine the Church of God, either to particular Nations, Churches, or Families, have made it far narrower than our Saviour ever meant it". For "whilst the mercies of God do promise us heaven, our conceits and opinions exclude us from that place. There must be, therefore, more than one St Peter: particular Churches and sects usurp the gates of heaven, and turn the key against each other; and thus we go to heaven against each others wills, conceits and opinions, and, with as much uncharity as ignorance, do err, I fear, in points not only of our own, but one anothers salvation."[2] The whole of Herbert's *De Veri-*

[1] Burton, *Anatomy of Melancholy*, part III, sect. IV, mem. I, subs. III.
[2] Browne, *Religio Medici*, part I.

tate is a rejection of the doctrine of exclusive salvation, and an attempt to find those common notions which are indisputably true and necessary for salvation, and may be accepted by men of all religions. As "le nombre (de ces principes communs) est déterminé et bien petit (dont je suis très certain)",[1] so particular Churches leave the truth, "les vérités certaines de la providence universelle de Dieu", when they enforce uncertain things as articles of faith. Only outside the doctrine of the common notions is there no salvation, for they alone are the true Catholic Church.[2]

In all things which are not fundamental these writers envisage the use of reason to arrive at such decisions as seem true; though in some cases reason must use the authority of revealed truth, and in other cases is subject to certain necessary restrictions. But compared with the subtleties of professional theologians, with their strict dependence upon the letter of Scripture, all these writers bring a refreshingly balanced and common-sense attitude into the discussion of theological problems, and allow reason to solve what the rival authorities from the Fathers and Scripture alone merely served to complicate and bring to a theological impasse. It follows, too, that they all share a certain scepticism about the activities of many theologians. "Ira hominis non implet justitiam Dei" as Bacon wrote on more than one occasion.[3] Especially, however, is this true of Selden, Browne, and Herbert. "Idolatry", said Selden, "is in a man's own

[1] Herbert, *op. cit.* p. 65. [2] *Ibid. passim.*
[3] Bacon, *Essays*: "Of Unity in Religion"; *An Advertisement touching the Controversies of the Church of England.*

thought, not in the opinion of another. Put a case I bow to the altar, why am I guilty of idolatry? because a stander-by thinks so? I am sure I do not believe the altar to be God; and the God I worship may be bowed to in all places, and at all times."[1] Again: "'twas an unhappy division that has been made between faith and works. Though in my intellect I may divide them, just as in the candle I know there is both light and heat; but yet put out the candle, and they are both gone; one remains not without the other: so 'tis betwixt faith and works."[2] Selden's aggressively sceptical attitude towards the activities of clerics is too well known to need illustration, but a representative reflection of his that "religion is made a juggler's paper; now 'tis a horse, now 'tis a lanthorn, now 'tis a brat, now 'tis a man. To serve ends religion is turned into all shapes",[3] has much affinity to Bacon's observation "that those which held and persuaded pressure of consciences were commonly interested therein themselves for their own ends".[4] When, further, Selden remarked that "the way to find out truth is by other's mistakings"[5] he was expressing the same belief in the profit that could be derived from a conflict of opinions that Browne maintained when he wrote that "they that endeavour to abolish vice, destroy also virtue; for contraries, though they destroy one another, are yet the life of one another".[6] Points not of faith, claims Browne, "may admit a free dispute", and may therefore be "observed according to the rules of my

---

[1] Selden, *op. cit.* "Idolatry."
[2] *Ibid.* "Faith and Works."
[3] *Ibid.* "Religion", 15.
[4] Bacon, *Essays*: "Of Unity."
[5] Selden, *op. cit.* "Truth", 2.
[6] Browne, *op. cit.* part II.

186

private reason, or the humour and fashion of my devotion; neither believing this because Luther affirmed it, or disapproving that, because Calvin hath disavouched it. I condemn not all things in the Council of Trent, nor approve all in the Synod of Dort. In brief, where the Scripture is silent the Church is my text; where that speaks, 'tis but my comment; where there is a joint silence of both I borrow not the rules of my religion from Rome or Geneva, but the dictates of my own reason."[1] Yet in the end Browne confesses that "having run through all sorts (of learning) he finds no rest in any: though our first studies and junior endeavours may stile us Peripatetics, Stoics, or Academics; yet I perceive the wisest heads prove, at last, almost all Sceptics, and stand like Janus in the field of knowledge".[2] Herbert, after expressing the belief that his few common notions are the only way to truth, which all philosophers and theologians must use, claimed that "les faineurs n'ayent donc plus recours à des noms magnifiques, pour autoriser leur erreurs; l'autorité est l'unique asile de l'ignorance".[3] And like Selden and Browne (and, in a later age, John Stuart Mill) Herbert appreciates the services that even error may render to truth, and the consequent necessity of a sympathetic approach in treating it. "Donc lorsque tu reprends quelqu'un d'un erreur, il ne faut pas rejeter toute l'opinion, puis qu'il y a quasi toujours quelque vérité dans toute sorte d'erreur, et par tant c'est ce qu'il faut examiner premièrement, et jusque où l'on convient. Et puis il faut montrer par nos questions et

---

[1] *Ibid.* part I.   [2] *Ibid.* part II.
[3] Herbert, *op. cit.* p. 208.

nos propres facultés comme quoi l'erreur s'est glissé; et en cette manière l'on quittera l'opiniâtreté, qui se trouve en ceux qui veulent soutenir leurs opinions à quelque prix que ce soit et l'on préparera le chemin pour toutes les autres vérités."[1] Herbert also suggests that in moral as distinguished from intellectual matters, certain men sin as the result of uncontrollable bodily dispositions. This does not mitigate the seriousness of their sins, but it does mean that they should be kindly dealt with.[2]

As these quotations from Herbert have indicated, and as we have already seen in the works of Chillingworth and Hales, the real solution which these lay latitudinarians suggest for the problems of persecution and a divided Christendom is that men should behave charitably and reasonably. In a pamphlet entitled *An advertisement touching the controversies of the Church of England*, Bacon urged upon both the Puritans and the bishops a greater mutual tolerance so that they might compound their differences over things which were not in themselves fundamental, and avoid factious and fanatical conduct. The controversies between them would close up naturally if both parties would but remember that the true bonds of unity are one faith and baptism and not one ceremony and policy; that Christ Himself proclaimed that he that is not against us is with us; that diversity of ceremonies sets forth the real unity of doctrine; that "religion hath parts belonging to time as well as to eternity"; that there is virtue in silence and slowness to speak, and that, therefore, men should refrain from violent humours, and recall the Apostle's

[1] Herbert, *op. cit.* p. 260.   [2] *Ibid.* p. 133.

advice and not enter into assertions but only counsel and advise. St Paul said: "Ego et non Dominus et secundum consilium meum", whereas men now too hastily say: "Non ego sed Dominus", "yea and bind it with a heavy denunciation of his judgments." Enlarging on this latter point, Bacon finds five offences in Church matters in which both Puritans and bishops must share the blame. First, the giving occasion of controversies, and the inconsiderate taking of occasion, under which head he rebukes the imperfections in the conversation and government of the bishops, the nature and humour of those persons who follow the names of things and of masters instead of the things themselves, who have an extreme detestation of some former heresy or corruption of the Church already acknowledged and convicted, and who urge a partial affectation and imitation of foreign Churches. Secondly, the extending of controversies to greater oppositions than were first in them; thirdly, the unbrotherly proceedings of each party to the other; fourthly, the measures taken by each party to draw their partisans to a more strait union with themselves to the disruption of the entire body. This is a fault peculiar to the Puritans, who not only call themselves alone godly, but forget that it is as wicked to shut where God has opened, as to open where God has shut. Fifthly, there is on both sides an inconvenient publishing of controversies (the significance of this will appear hereafter). This is very detailed and wise, and distributes praise and blame with an impartial hand. It should not be forgotten that in *Certain Considerations touching the better pacification of the Church of England*

Bacon had already advocated certain concessions to the Puritans, for the question as he saw it is "not of toleration by convenience, which may encourage disobedience, but by law which may give a liberty".

Selden, believing that "a man can think no otherwise than he does think",[1] and that "he is a poor divine that cannot sever the good from the bad" and therefore requires the destruction of much good learning in the suppression of "popish books",[2] believed also that while "they talk much of settling religion: religion is well enough settled already, if we would let it alone".[3] He protests against the wresting and misuse of Scripture, against picking texts out of their contexts, for example, and deplores the practice of the level of the controversy in religious disputes being set by the least mannerly. "In matters of religion, to be ruled by one that writes against his adversary, and throws all the dirt he can in his face, is, as if in point of good manners a man should be governed by one whom he sees at cuffs with another, and thereupon thinks himself bound to give the next man he meets a box on the ear."[4] Burton, seeing the cause of so much misery and bloodshed in the perversity of Papists and schismatics, and that "no greater concord, no greater discord than that which proceeds from religion"[5] suggests, on occasions, that the remedy lies with the individual. "This hatred, malice, faction and desire of revenge, invented first all those racks, and wheels, strappadoes, brazen bulls, feral engines, prisons,

---

[1] Selden, *op. cit.* "Opinion", 4.   [2] *Ibid.* "Books", 4.
[3] *Ibid.* "Religion", 18.   [4] *Ibid.* "Religion", 11.
[5] Burton, *op. cit.* part III, sect. IV, mem. I, subs. III.

inquisitions, severe laws to macerate and torment one another. How happy might we be, and end our time with blessed days and sweet content, if we could contain ourselves, and, as we ought to do, put up injuries, learn humility, meekness, patience, forget and forgive, as in God's word we are enjoined, compose such small controversies amongst ourselves, moderate our passions in this kind, and think better of others, as Paul would have us, than of ourselves: be of like affection one towards another, and not avenge ourselves, but have peace with all men!"[1] As Sir Thomas Browne believed that the "leaven and ferment of all, not only civil but religious actions, is wisdom",[2] so, after a confession of his personal tolerance, his inability to conceive "why a difference in opinion should divide our affection", he states, more generally, that "controversies, disputes and argumentations, both in philosophy and in divinity, if they meet with discreet and peaceable natures, do not infringe the laws of charity. In all disputes, so much as there is of passion, so much as there is of nothing to the purpose; for then reason, like a bad hound, spends upon a false scent, and forsakes the question first started. And this is one reason why controversies are never determined; for although they be amply proposed, they are scarce at all handled, they do swell with unnecessary digressions."[3]

This protest of a scholarly mind against the violent and popular handling of controversies to the prejudice of truth has been noticed before in the works of Hales,

---

[1] *Ibid*. part I, sect. II, mem. III, subs. VIII.
[2] Browne, *op. cit*. part I.   [3] *Ibid*. part II.

and is repeated with a marked unanimity by Bacon, Selden and Burton as well as (more explicitly than in the above quotation) by Browne. Selden uses the same simile as Hales to express his opinion. "In troubled water you can scarce see your face, or see it very little, till the water be quiet and stand still. So in troubled times you can see little truth; when times are quiet and settled then truth appears."[1] Burton shares Hales' dislike of the prodigious number of worthless books that are printed. Though he modestly confesses to have added to the number, Democritus confesses too that "'tis most true, tenet insanabile multos scribendi cacoethes, and there is no end of writing of books, as the wise-man found of old, in this scribbling age especially, wherein the number of books is without number (as a worthy man saith), presses be oppressed, and out of an itching humour, that every man hath to show himself, desirous of fame and honour (scribimus indocti doctique—) he will write no matter what, and scrape together it boots not whence....By which means it comes to pass that not only libraries and shops are full of our putid papers, but every close-school and jakes."[2] Bacon, too, as we have seen, protested against the inconvenient publishing of controversies, and Sir Thomas Browne suggested the same remedy as Hales. "'Tis not a melancholy utinam of my own, but the desires of better heads, that there were a general synod; not to unite the incompatible difference of religion, but for the benefit of learning, to reduce it as it lay at first, in a few and solid

---

[1] Selden, *op. cit.* "Truth", 3.
[2] Burton, *op. cit.* "Democritus to Reader."

authors; and to condemn to the fire those swarms and millions of rhapsodies, begotten only to distract and abuse the weaker judgments of scholars, and to maintain the trade and mystery of typographers."[1] Browne's expressed motive in this plea for what Hales called "theological pandects" is important. It is not to obviate diversity of belief, but to ensure that controversies shall not waste themselves or their hearers. Nor is this motive peculiar to Browne, for any restrictive measures advocated by these writers in consequence of these beliefs are not directed against any particular opinion, but against the incompetent or needlessly violent expression of it. "Every man", as Browne said, "is not a proper champion for truth, nor fit to take up the gauntlet in the cause of verity: many, from the ignorance of these maxims, and an inconsiderable zeal unto truth, have too rashly charged the troops of error, and remain as trophies unto the enemies of truth."[2] Moreover, as every man is not a proper champion of truth, Bacon, Selden and Browne agree that in some cases he is no fit hearer of the controversies from which it is to emerge. Bacon protests against all men being allowed to hear controversies, not only because the Apostle advised the weak in faith to be shut from doubtful disputations, but more especially because "whatsoever be pretended the people is no meet arbitrator, but rather the quiet, modest and private assemblies and conferences of the learned".[3] Selden expressed his dislike of every one interpreting Scripture

[1] Browne, *op. cit.* part I.   [2] *Ibid.*
[3] Bacon, *Advert. touching the Controvs. of the C. of E.*

as they list. "Scrutamini Scripturas. These two words have undone the world", and he enumerates the laws restraining the reading and interpretation thereof. His desire is, however, not that it should be confined to the clergy, but to the learned, for, indeed, "laymen have best interpreted the hard places in the Bible".[1] Browne contemns and laughs at the multitude—not only the base people but also the "plebeian heads" amongst the gentry—as the "great enemy of reason, virtue and religion".[2] Except in the case of Bacon, these opinions represent personal wishes rather than considered statements on public policy. But, as with Hales, they are, nevertheless, a restriction on absolute liberty of thought, and do indicate that, although it may be true that "plebeian heads" have little of value to contribute to the sum of objective truth, these authors have yet to see that liberty of discussion, however incompetently employed, may increase the sum of truth in the "plebeian head" itself.

On the more particular problems of Church and State there is less unanimity amongst these writers, and it therefore becomes necessary to consider their views separately. Francis Bacon had too empirical a mind to lay down religious liberty as a general rule, even had he believed in it. By method Bacon, in politics, is of the school of Machiavelli: "il n'a rien fait pour les principes",[3] and his views on Church and State, therefore, emerge less as statements of general theory, as from his

---

[1] Selden, *op. cit.* "Bible", 4, 5, 6, 7.
[2] Browne, *op. cit.* part II.
[3] Janet, *Hist. de la Science Politique*, II, 101.

consideration of particular problems requiring a particular solution. In *Certain Considerations touching the better pacification of the Church of England*, for example, enumerating certain concessions calculated to allay the discontent of the Puritans, Bacon is led to assert that it is untrue to believe that it is against good policy to innovate in Church matters, for if the civil state is frequently reformed in Parliament why not the ecclesiastical? It is further untrue to believe that "reformation must be after one platform". Church government should vary with time and place, as civil governments do. Substance and doctrine alone are immutable; all the rest, rites, ceremonies, hierarchies, policies are left at large. Bacon's attitude to political and ecclesiastical problems of this nature is much conditioned by the belief that in many things we must seek "non quod optimum sed ex bonis quid proximum".[1] In a paper entitled "Considerations touching the Queen's service in Ireland" written in 1601 in a letter to Mr Secretary Cecil, for example, he advocates, in Ireland, a toleration of religion for a time, accompanied by some good and definite instruction, since they are not yet fit to receive the reformed religion. He also urges that the toleration shall not be definite, except in some principal towns, after the manner of the French edicts. It should be observed that Bacon here assumes the acceptance of the reformed religion by the Irish, and not toleration, to be the desired end of policy, and, indeed, he only accepts the latter as a temporary expedient. Bacon approved

[1] Bacon, *Advert. touching the Controvs. of the C. of E.*

of the penal laws,[1] and his pleas for mutual tolerance and concession were made with reference only to the controversies within the Church of England. He is always prepared to adapt means to ends, and even in *Certain Considerations touching the better pacification of the Church of England* he makes no attempt to claim toleration as a right. It is merely suggested as perhaps the best way to Christian unity.

In the essay "Of Unity in Religion", however, Bacon does make a general statement of his views on the question of Church and State. His first sentence, asserting religion to be "the chief bond of human society", indicates that he has no tendency towards the separatist idea of toleration, that he is not, like John Earle's sceptic in religion, mistrustful of "this connexion of the commonweal and divinity and fears it may be an arch practice of State". He does not, therefore, disallow the use of force in religious matters, but only certain uses of it. There are, he asserts, three swords to be considered: the spiritual sword, the temporal sword and Mahomet's sword, which is the propagating of religion by wars or persecution. Of these, the first two may legitimately be used to maintain religion, but not the third "except it be in cases of overt scandal, blasphemy, or intermixture of practice against the state". The remainder of the essay is not an attack on the use of the temporal sword in religion, i.e. the use of the civil authority of the magistrate, because Bacon explicitly allows this, but against the use of unauthorized force by

[1] This is clear from *A certificate to his majesty touching the projects of Sir Stephen Proctor relating to Penal Laws.*

either prince or people. Such a use of force in religion as was exhibited in the Massacre of St Bartholomew's Eve, or in the powder treason in England is against the Christian religion. Bacon therefore insists that unity in religion must not be attained by *any* means. Certain methods, even though they might be successful, are forbidden. For example, men must not dissolve and deface the laws of charity and of human society, they should not so consider men as Christians as to forget that they are men, nor dash the first table against the second (i.e. we should not fail in our duty to our neighbour while doing that to God). In other words Bacon admits that there are greater evils in religion than mere lack of unity. Further, although the use of the temporal sword has "its due office and place" in the maintenance of the Christian religion, yet it is only to be drawn in cases of great circumspection. It is (by implication) not the best way to unity, which lies rather in those beliefs of Bacon which we have already examined and with which he opens the present essay. In fundamentals men should agree; and allow liberty in non-fundamentals. This will be more easily achieved if men would avoid certain kinds of profitless controversies. But just as Bacon was not prepared to have unity at any price, so he rejects peace at any price. The unity achieved must not be such as is "grounded but upon an implicit ignorance, for all colours will agree in the dark"; nor must it be such as is "pieced upon a direct admission of contraries in fundamental points: for truth and falsehood, in such things, are like the iron and clay in the toes of Nebuchadnezzar's image; they may cleave, but they will not incorporate".

As, therefore, Bacon rejects certain means to unity as unlawful, so he rejects certain kinds of unity as not to be desired, even though they should be obtained by legitimate means.

Although it was the practice of John Selden to inscribe the words "Above all Liberty" upon the fly-leaf of his books, his interest was in a technical legal liberty, and parliamentary privilege, rather than in any general principle of religious toleration. On 11 February 1629, for example, Selden made a speech in the Commons over a petition of certain printers, complaining that Laud had refused to license books which the printers described as orthodox at the same time as he had licensed Arminian and Popish books, and that the printers, acting in defiance of this decision, had been punished by the High Commission. The petition was presented in the middle of the struggle between King and Parliament over Bishop Neile and the Declaration prefixed to the Articles, and its issue was in effect to decide which party in Church and State should succeed in silencing the other. But Selden made no general plea for religious liberty. He based his support of the petition upon the common law, and contented himself with attacking the prerogative powers of the Star Chamber. "There is no law to prevent the printing of any book in England, only a decree in the Star Chamber", and "therefore, that a man should be fined and imprisoned and his goods taken from him, is a great invasion on the liberty of the subject."[1]

[1] Cobbett, *Parliamentary History*, p. 463. Gardiner, *History of England*, VII, 51.

Selden's attitude to the problems of Church and State is entirely conditioned by his Erastianism (in the popular and more usually accepted sense of the term). The measure of all problems, both civil and ecclesiastical, is, for him, the interests and welfare of the State, and more especially of the common law by which it ought to be governed. *The History of Tythes*, which was published in 1618, is in effect a defence of the common law against ecclesiastical usurpations. Although Selden was afterwards forced to disclaim (as, technically, he could) any intention of attacking the divine right of tithes,[1] he argued, in his history, that there was no proof whatsoever that tithes had ever been claimed of right during the first four hundred years of the Christian era; and in treating of their subsequent history he showed that the practices had been so various, and had been so completely subjected to local customs, and to the laws of various European nations, that the payment had in reality been accepted by the clergy from the State with whatsoever limitations the civil authorities had chosen to impose.[2] In *Table Talk* Selden's Erastianism is the common factor to nearly all his observations. From a brief account of the dispute at the beginning of Queen Elizabeth's reign between Protestants and Papists of which Sir Nicholas Bacon was the judge, Selden remarks: "For so religion was brought into these kingdoms, so it has been continued, and so it may be cast out, when the State pleases."[3] "The State still makes

[1] *Vide* Selden: "Of my purpose and end in writing the history of tythes." Letter to Marquess of Buckingham, 5 May 1620.

[2] Gardiner, *op. cit.* III, 253.

[3] Selden, *op. cit.* "Bishops out", 13.

THE LAY LATITUDINARIANS

religion and receives into it what will best agree with it."[1] "There is", therefore, "no such thing as spiritual jurisdiction; all is civil; the Church's is the same with the Lord Mayor's."[2] The power of Bishops and Presbyters thus comes to be much the same. If Bishops were abolished they would have to be replaced by something else,[3] and "besides all jurisdiction is temporal; and in no Church but they have some jurisdiction or other. The question then is reduced to magis and minus; they meddle more in one church than another."[4]

Selden thus came to believe in religious liberty, as he believed in most other things, only in so far as it conduces to the safety and the welfare of the State. For, on the one hand, he insists upon the danger of pretending conscience against law ("except in some cases where haply we may"),[5] the danger that attends any alteration in religion, "because we know not where it will stay",[6] and the importance of keeping divines within their bounds, "for fear of breeding confusion since there now be so many religions on foot".[7] While, on the other hand, he believes that, as neither the Church nor Scripture is the judge of religion, but the State,[8] so "'tis to no purpose to labour to reconcile religions when the interest of princes will not suffer it. 'Tis well if they could be reconciled so far, that they should not cut one another's throats."[9] Selden here seems to envisage the

---

[1] Selden, *op. cit.* "Religion", 8.
[2] *Ibid.* "Jurisdiction", 1. See also "Excommunication", 4.
[3] *Ibid.* "Bishops out", 12. [4] *Ibid.* "Bishops in", 5.
[5] *Ibid.* "Conscience", 3. [6] *Ibid.* "Religion", 6.
[7] *Ibid.* "Religion", 13. [8] *Ibid.* "Religion", 7.
[9] *Ibid.* "Religion", 12.

State preventing religious sects resorting to violence in so far as its interests will allow it. If the interests of the State are civil peace and liberty, as for Selden they were, this is clearly the political theory of the latitudinarian. Selden's latitudinarian observations, which we have noticed heretofore, sprang from his desire to find a solution to pointless disputes which disturbed the State. But if liberty and the interests of the State should conflict, it is the State, and not a general absolute liberty, which is his primary concern. He expressly rejects the toleration of Papists because the Pope is their king.[1] To-day Selden's principles would be as detrimental to religious liberty as they were favourable to it in his own day.

In *The Anatomy of Melancholy* Burton considers toleration as the cure of religious melancholy, but only largely to reject it. To "purge the world of idolatry and superstition" would require the advent of Christ, for, in general, men are "so refractory, self-conceited, obstinate, so firmly addicted to that religion in which they have been bred and brought up, that no persuasion, no terror, no persecution can divert them. The consideration of which hath induced many commonwealths to suffer them to enjoy their consciences as they will themselves." Burton considers the testimonies of those who have favoured complete toleration, including that of the Socinians; and of those, especially the Roman Catholics, who will tolerate infidels and pagans but not heretics. In the controversy between Calvin, Beza and Castellion, however, he supports the two former and

[1] *Ibid.* "Pope", 7.

explicitly rejects complete toleration. "Castalio &c., Martin Bellius and his companions maintained this opinion (that no man for religion or conscience be put to death) not long since in France, whose error is confuted by Beza in a just volume. The medium is best and that which Paul prescribes, Gal. vi. 1. 'If any man shall fall by occasion, to restore such a one with the spirit of meekness, by all fair means, gentle admonitions': but if that will not take place, 'post unam et alteram admonitionem haereticum devita', he must be excommunicate, as Paul did by Hymenaus delivered over to Satan. 'Immedicabile vulnus ense recidendum est.' As Hippocrates said in Physic, I may well say in Divinity, 'quae ferro non curantur, ignis curat'. For the vulgar, restrain them by laws, mulcts, burn their books, forbid their conventicles: for when the cause is taken away, the effect will soon cease." As for "prophets, dreamers, and such rude silly fellows", Burton would have them cured by a trick, or put in Bedlam.[1] Of the writers considered in this chapter Burton is the most distant from the idea of religious liberty.

Sir Thomas Browne in *Religio Medici*, on the other hand, is by much the closest. Browne's idea of toleration is essentially the product of his own personal tolerance which he exhibits throughout his work. Though he "dares without usurpation assume the honourable stile of a Christian", yet his zeal therein does not "so far make me forget the general charity I owe unto humanity, as rather to hate than pity Turks, Infidels, and (what is worse) Jews; rather contenting myself to enjoy

[1] Burton, *op. cit.* part III, sect. IV, mem. I, subs. v.

that happy stile, than maligning those who refuse so glorious a title".[1] Browne's condemnation of persecution is explicit. "The Jew is obstinate in all fortune; the persecution of fifteen hundred years hath but confirmed them in their error; they have already endured whatsoever may be inflicted, and have suffered in a bad cause even to the condemnation of their enemies. Persecution is a bad and indirect way to plant religion: it hath been the unhappy method of angry devotions, not only to confirm honest religion, but wicked heresies and extravagant opinions." Although persecution was "the first stone and basis of our faith", Browne insists that "'tis not in the power of every honest faith to proceed thus far, or pass to heaven through the flames", and that as "the leaven and ferment of all, not only civil law but religious actions, is wisdom", so it is folly to expose one's life over a trifle. "I would not perish upon a ceremony, politic points, or indifferency."[2] More explicit views on the problems of Church and State than this Browne does not vouchsafe us. But in this he is thoroughly representative of the latitudinarian tolerationist, to whom tolerance is always the best and surest way to toleration.

There is no explicit discussion of toleration or persecution in Herbert's *De Veritate*, but the whole tenor of the book would seem to condemn persecution by implication. We cannot, says Herbert, take truth upon the authority of others, for each man must answer for himself before the sovereign judge. It is essential therefore so to establish the fundamentals and foundations of

---

[1] Browne, *op. cit.* part I.   [2] *Ibid.*

religion, that they may be clear to all, and capable of acceptance by all: we must find the common notions which are the quintessence of religious belief to all men.[1] Now we have seen that Chillingworth had been much occupied in formulating the few fundamentals which are necessary to salvation, and had arrived at the conclusion that, although it was impossible to give a precise catalogue of fundamentals, yet the Apostles' Creed contained within itself all necessary points of mere belief, and the Scripture all things necessary to salvation. In two ways Herbert proceeds beyond Chillingworth. First, he gives a catalogue of the five fundamental beliefs necessary to salvation. These are, in brief, that there is a Supreme Power; that this sovereign power must be worshipped; that the good ordering or disposition of the faculties of man constitutes the principal or best part of divine worship; that all vices and crimes should be expiated and effaced by repentance; and that there are rewards and punishments after this life.[2] Secondly, Herbert regards this catalogue of fundamentals as truths which will be acceptable not only to Christians, but to all men, irrespective of their more specific religious beliefs.[3] It follows, therefore, that Herbert's work was the most extensive attack on the doctrine of exclusive salvation that was published during the early seventeenth century, and was one of the most distinguished attempts to solve the problem which had been posed in Donne's sonnet. "Je n'ai pas fait voir le

---

[1] Herbert, *op. cit.* p. 51.
[2] Willey, B., *The Seventeenth-Century Background*, p. 121 *seq.*
[3] *Ibid.* p. 122.

jour à ce livre pour émouvoir des controverses, mais plutôt pour en donner la solution, ou du moins pour les abolir."[1] How far Herbert accepted the implications of the *De Veritate* on the subject of persecution is difficult to estimate. His *Autobiography* certainly does not reveal him devoting his life to the cause, and his yearning for praise from whatever quarter made his opinions, on occasion, very volatile. Thus on 14 March 1635 he sent Charles a paper of observations on the necessity of vesting the supremacy of the Church in the ruler of the State, and the King sent the document to Laud, with whom Herbert was on familiar terms. But at the same time he also informed Panzani, the Papal emissary,[2] that in his *History of Henry VIII* he intended to favour the theories of the Papacy, and offered to submit the *De Veritate* to the Pope's criticism.[3] The *Autobiography*, however, does show Herbert interceding in France as English Ambassador, to persuade the King against religious wars, though it is not clear whether this sprang from specifically tolerant motives, or from the more partisan desire to protect his co-religionists.

The latitudinarian position was also expressed in verse during this period. George Wither in *Britain's Remembrancer*, published in 1628, expressed views similar in essentials to those we have found in certain prose writers. Wither was a man of strong views, but wholly devoted to moderation and tolerance. His condemnation of factious spirits, of those who

---

[1] Herbert, *op. cit.*: "Au lecteur."
[2] *Vide* chap. VIII.
[3] *D.N.B.*

> ...Suppose that no man's doctrine saves
> The soul of anyone, unless he raves,
> And rears aloud, and flings, and hurleth so
> As if his arms he quite away would throw

led him to a characteristically latitudinarian position, save that unlike most latitudinarians he conceived it to be his duty to oppose all governments rather than quietly to accept any. God has made necessary truth clear, and therefore it is unnecessary so to pry further into His mysteries as to make Christianity into an inflexible dogmatic system.

> God never yet did bid us take in hand
> To publish that which none can understand:
> Much less affecteth he a man should mutter
> Rude sounds of that, whose depth he cannot utter.
>
> .   .   .   .
>
> For that which man to man is bound to show,
> Are such plain Truths, as we by word may know.

Although Wither thought that the true Church of Christ lay between the extremes of the English parties, he professed himself willing to conform to any ecclesiastical system provided it preserved the fundamentals. During the period of the Civil War and even after the Restoration Wither made further important contributions to the idea of religious liberty which he had already formulated thus early.

Like that of many latitudinarians Wither's tolerance sprang originally from a certain scepticism about human beliefs, realizing as he did how much they were based on chance and irrationality. But no latitudinarian felt this quite so strongly as Francis Quarles to whom it was "glorious misery to be born a man". But even Quarles never allowed his pessimism, which could be morbid at times, to destroy his belief that men must seek for the truth by the use of the reason and the free will with which God has endowed them. Though "opinion might thwart opinion" he maintained firmly that scepticism honestly held was a surer way to truth than intemperate bigotry. Faith is to be found not in authority, but in a man's own mind

> ...looking down into my troubled breast,
> The magazine of wounds, I found him there.[1]

And therefore to tyrannize over reason by persecution is wrong.

> Man in himself's a little World, Alone,
> His soul's the court, or high Imperial Throne,
> Wherein as Empress, sits the Understanding
> Gently directing, yet with awe Commanding
> Her Handmaid's will.[2]

Quarles warned the clergy against persecution lest they should root out the young wheat with the tares.

> Judge not too fast: this tree that doth appear
> So barren, may be fruitful the next year.
>
> .   .   .   .
>
> A Saul today, may prove a Paul, the next.[3]

Factious and intolerant sects Quarles permitted to be "nipped in the bud", as all latitudinarians allow the use of civil force in religious matters for the purpose of maintaining religious peace. But once they are estab-

---

[1] Quarles, *Works*, ed. Grosart, III, 86.
[2] *Ibid.* II, 28.　　　　　　　　　[3] *Ibid.* II, 208.

lished "it is wisdom not to oppose them with too strong a hand; lest in suppressing one, there arise two: A soft current is soon stopped; but a strong stream resisted, breaks into many, or overwhelms all."[1]

It is interesting to observe that both Ben Jonson and William Drummond of Hawthornden, who were well acquainted with each other, insisted upon the impotence of the sword ultimately to destroy or suppress the works of the pen. In an "Apologetical Letter" from William Drummond to the Earl of Ancrum which was written with the intention that it should come to the eyes of Charles himself, Drummond urged upon the King a policy of tolerance and moderation in dealing with the *Supplication* of June 1633, which, connected with Balmerino's name, Charles regarded as subversive and libellous.[2] The tenor of Drummond's counsel is that "in a matter of calumny and reproach with subjects, a Prince can do nothing more fitting his own fame and reputation than to slight and contemn them, as belonging nothing to him; and 'twere better to neglect than to be too curious in searching after the authors". But, more specifically, he indicates the futility of attempting to suppress them by methods of violence. "Is this the way to suppress and hide them? To imprison, arraign, banish, execute the persons near whom they are found? Or is it not rather to turn them a piece of the story of the time to make such a noise about them, and by seeking to avoid the smoke to fall into the fire?" "Writings which

[1] *Ibid.* I, 16. See Jordan, *The Development of Religious Toleration in England*, II, 352–6.
[2] Gardiner, *op. cit.* VII, 295.

we scorn and make none account, of themselves vanish
and turn into nought. If we chase and fret it would
appear that we have been therein touched, and vively
see in them our own faults and misdemeanours taxed
and laid open." Those, therefore, who have "busied the
Prince to condemn others by power (a minister of their
attempts) and not purge himself to posterity", are
greatly mistaken; "for such a paper should have been
answered by a pen not by an axe". "No Prince, how
great soever, can abolish pens, nor will memorials of
ages be extinguished by present power; the posterity
rendering to everyone his due honour and blame."[1]

In *Sejanus* Ben Jonson makes Cremutius Cordus and
his defenders express exactly similar sentiments. Cordus
is attacked by Sejanus, through Tiberius, because he is
the author of certain annals which assert that Brutus was
the last of the Romans. In his defence Cordus asserts
that true obloquies are best despised, not punished by
force, for so the great emperors have treated them.

> The epigrams of Bibaculus and Catullus
> Are read, full stuft with spite of both the Caesars;
> Yet deified Julius, and no less Augustus,
> Both bore them, and contemn'd them: I not know
> Promptly to speak it, whether done with more
> Temper, or wisdom; for such obloquies
> If they despised be, they die supprest;
> But if with rage acknowledg'd, they are confest.
> The Greeks I slip, whose license not alone,
> But also lust did 'scape unpunished:
> Or where some one, by chance, exception took,
> He words with words revenged.

[1] W. Drummond of Hawthornden, *A History of Scotland, etc.*, p. 358.

And when the court ordered Cordus' books to be burnt, Arruntius cries, in words so similar to those afterwards used by Drummond that the latter may well have had them in mind when he wrote his letter:

> Let them be burnt! O, how ridiculous
> Appears the senate's brainless diligence,
> Who think they can, with present powers, extinguish
> The memory of all succeeding times!

To which Sabinus adds:

> 'Tis true: when, contrary, the punishment
> Of wit, doth make the authority increase.
> Nor do they aught, that use this cruelty
> Of interdiction, and this rage of burning,
> But purchase to themselves rebuke and shame,
> And to the writers an eternal name.[1]

Neither Jonson nor Drummond considers here explicitly religious liberty, but the implications of their observations to it are clear, as well as to the practice of which Shakespeare confessed himself tired in his sixty-sixth sonnet,[2] of

> right perfection wrongfully disgrac'd,
> And strength by limping sway disabled,
> And art made tongue-tied by authority,
> And folly (doctor-like) controlling skill,
> And simple truth miscalled simplicity,
> And captive good attending captain ill.

[1] Ben Jonson, *Sejanus*, Act III, Sc. I.
[2] Masson, *Life of Milton*, III, 100, points out the implications of this sonnet.

CHAPTER VIII

ROMAN CATHOLIC THEORY

THE historic Catholic theory of theological persecution ensured, as we have seen, that the contribution of Catholicism to the idea of toleration
should be small, and at best incidental. The practical
exigences of the position of Roman Catholics, as well as
their desire to recover England for the faith, led them
to consider the question, and their pleas for toleration
were considered by Anglican divines more worthy of
explicit theoretical refutation than those of any others.
This was not due to the intrinsic merit of their ideas,
but to the success and menace of the Counter-Reformation abroad, and to the political dangers of Catholicism
which, in the light of the Gunpowder Plot, seemed at
the beginning of James' reign as real as the Puritan
danger was potential.

From the literature I have examined it would seem
that the Catholic approach to the problem of toleration
went through three main phases during the years 1603–
39. The first phase extends from 1603 to 1608, and may
be characterized as the period in which Catholics hoped
for some direct grant of toleration by the King. There
had been many rumours both before and immediately
on James' accession to the throne that the King was
preparing to grant a toleration, and James had further

encouraged these hopes when he ordered, at his accession, a temporary suspension of the penal laws.[1] It was of this indulgence that Catholics were anxious to make permanent advantage, and they plead the cause of toleration for themselves largely on the political grounds that characterized the English Seculars towards the end of Elizabeth's reign. But this first phase may itself be subdivided into two. From 1603 to 1605 the Catholic pleas that I have examined all plead for a positive toleration. From 1605 to 1608, on the other hand, the period which succeeded the Gunpowder Plot, they are more directed against the increasing of the penal laws, than craving for greater indulgences.[2]

The *Catholics Supplication*[3] of 1603 to which Gabriel Powel replied is clearly the work of the English Seculars, and the arguments they present for toleration are almost wholly political. They profess their duty, service and loyalty to the King. The late Queen they served loyally despite persecution, and they beg the King to consider what they would not do to live free in the King's favour. They cite the toleration of Protestants, who domineered under the late Queen, of Puritans, who have crept up

[1] The Rumours spread even to Ireland, *vide* Bishop of Dublin to King. 4 June 1603, *Irish. Cal.* 1603–6, 70.

[2] There must be many Catholic pleas for toleration which are not extant, or which I have not had the opportunity to examine. But there seems to be no reason to suppose that the ensuing literature is not representative. Catholic pleas seem in most cases to have survived where they were subsequently embodied in an Anglican reply to them.

[3] *The Catholics Supplication unto the King's Majesty for Toleration of Catholic Religion in England: with short notes or animadversions in the margin: whereunto is annexed parallelwise a Supplicatory Counterpoyse of the Protestants*...1603.

apace, and of "atheists and politicians", "who were bred upon their brawls and contentions in matters of faith", and ask why Catholics too may not be tolerated, because they certainly cannot be suppressed. They point out the beneficial effects of toleration: that peace in France has resulted from it, that trade would revive and taxes become less, and that thereby the favour of Catholic princes abroad might be gained. They praise the Catholic religion, not merely as the religion "venerable for antiquity" which was professed by the King's predecessors, but as the only religion which teaches obedience for conscience sake, whereas Puritans only pretend obedience. They profess their allegiance to the King and pray for favour. The whole controversy shows no glimmer of an appreciation of the wider issues of toleration. The *Catholics Supplication* is a wholly *ex parte* plea for indulgence, and makes no claims for a persecuted conscience.

A Supplication to the Kings most excellent Majesty of 1604,[1] however, which was answered by both Powel and an anonymous writer whom certain evidence suggests to be Matthew Sutclife, Dean of Exeter,[2] though covering much the same ground, was more able and cogent. The real concern of the supplicants is with indulgence for themselves. Their claims are modest enough. They seek

[1] *A Supplication to the Kings most excellent Majesty: wherein several reasons of state and religion are briefly touched...*1604.

[2] In Powel's reply to this pamphlet (*vide infra*) he indicates that this is the fourth supplication of the Catholics, and that it has already been replied to by Dr Sutclife. A later work of Dr Sutclife also reproduces phrases and arguments which had already appeared in the anonymous reply to this present supplication.

neither churches nor maintenance, but merely revision of the penal laws, and licence to practise their religion in private houses. In support of this claim they adduce the usual political arguments, but amongst them some that would seem to indicate that they envisaged a toleration for all sects. General toleration of conscience, they say, would induce all men to strive how best to serve the King from whom they have thereby received so much. Mercy and truth should preserve a king, and the love of his subjects is a king's best defence. Toleration would cause thousands of his subjects to love him. By the doctrine of Protestants—and here they cite the early Protestant pleas against persecution—toleration is neither hurtful nor unlawful. After a long praise and proof of the truth of the Catholic religion, the supplicants cite the toleration of the Puritans who differ in thirty-two points from the "Protestants" (i.e. the Anglicans). They urge, moreover, that Catholics are punished for non-attendance at Church, which is truly a point of religion with them—"a true real obligation of mere conscience"—and in this respect "an erroneous conscience bindeth as strongly, and under equal pain, as doth the conscience that is best and most rightly informed". They desire merely to distinguish their eternal from their temporal lord, and to prefer obedience to the one to obedience to the other (for to obey a prince against God would be no obedience at all). There is some appreciation of the wider problems of toleration in this—the respective allegiances of Church and State and the obligations of conscience; but the supplicants have no real belief in their statements as universal principles. They are convenient means to a predetermined end, and the supplicants adduce elsewhere the argument that the Anglican Church would benefit from the toleration of Roman Catholics because both could then combine to suppress the Puritans. The *Supplication* presents many advantages which might accrue from toleration of themselves, but few real reasons against persecution, and certainly none that they would have regarded as universally valid.

A difference of interpretation as to what constituted mere matter of religion lay behind much Catholic and Anglican polemic in the early seventeenth century. In 1606 Sutclife issued another reply to a Catholic petition for toleration, which he called *The Petition Apologetical of Lay Papists...contradicted, examined, glozzed and refuted.* The *Petition Apologetical* of the lay Papists was a petition of 1604 which attempted to persuade the King not to confirm the Act against Recusants of 4 June.[1] On both sides familiar arguments are recapitulated, but the *Petition*, quoting Burghley's *Execution of Justice* and the practice of Elizabeth, suggests a form of submission and allegiance which was later to be carried out by the Oath of Allegiance of 1606. Though the oath of 1606 only partially fulfilled the petitioners' plea that they should be made "as entire and absolute Englishmen as other subjects of all professions", yet it was their own willingness to compromise with the State as to what constituted mere matter of religion that facilitated this concession. The need for priests, and abstention from church, they in-

[1] Gardiner, *History of England*, 1603–42, I, 203.

sisted upon—but not the indirect temporal power of the Papacy or any doctrines of deposition.

To the Jesuits, however, both these doctrines continued to remain essential. Robert Parsons, in his *Treatise tending to Mitigation towards Catholic subjects in England*, published in 1607, denies that those who compromise the Jesuit conception of Catholicism are Catholics at all, and defends the indirect temporal power of the Papacy by natural reason and Christian principles.[1] But even Parsons, having apparently abandoned, under the threat of the persecution which succeeded the Gunpowder Plot, all hopes of Catholic dominance in England, is prepared to make some concessions. Under Elizabeth Parsons had pleaded nobly the rights of conscience, but he had never been willing to compromise his views for the sake of a mere toleration. Now, however, he urges not only that to extirpate all Catholics from the kingdom would be prejudicial to his Majesty's estate, but that "the doctrine of the incompatibility of Protestant and Catholic people together, under the government of his Majesty of Great Britain is not only false and erroneous in itself...but pernicious also to the commonwealth, prejudicial to his Majesty's both comfort and safety, hurtful to the State, seditious against peace, scandalous to the hearers, offensive to foreign nations that live under princes of different religions, both Catholic and Protestant, and hateful finally to the ears of all moderate,

---

[1] *Op. cit.* Preface. He argues that there must somewhere be some control over rulers, and that spiritual things must not be sacrificed to temporal. On this all Catholics agree, though he admits diversity of opinions as to its practical operation.

peaceable and prudent people: and is on the other side no ways profitable, needful, expedient or convenient".[1] As the Catholic contribution to this settlement Parsons urged Catholics to abstain from rebellion, which he characterized as utterly unlawful, and under certain specified circumstances not to make use of equivocation and mental reservation even where it was spiritually lawful. The Catholic practice of equivocation had tended to make their oaths worthless, and Parsons urges Catholics to avoid its use (except where truth, plainly stated, would endanger others) to prevent further misunderstandings and calumnies.[2] Parsons' concessions, however, are only in practice, and not in theory, and his pamphlet remains a statement which he would not have made had circumstances been different. He emphasizes constantly that the policy he is advocating is the result of the exigences of the situation, and that Catholics must refrain from certain acts not because they are unlawful, but because they are not expedient. "Omnia mihi licent; sed omnia non expediunt." It is not, therefore, surprising to find that there was no diminution, as the result of this work, in Protestant fears and suspicions.

From 1608 to 1615 Catholic polemic is entirely occupied with the controversy over the Oath of Allegiance. Thereby Catholic opinion was strictly divided into the Jesuit and regular party which rejected the oath according to the instructions in the Pope's breves, and the smaller and less influential seculars who accepted it. James' reply in his *Apology for the Oath of Allegiance* to

[1] Parsons, *Treatise tending to Mitigation*, chap. I.
[2] *Ibid.* Conclusion. Chap. XIII.

the Pope's breves, which asserted that "the integrity of the Catholic religion permitteth not Catholics to take such an oath", produced a controversy of European extent. Led by Cardinal Bellarmine under the pseudonym Matthaeus Tortus, the Jesuits defended the indirect temporal power of the Papacy, and the Papal power of deposition, and urged Catholics not to take an oath in which, as Parsons wrote, "both civil and ecclesiastical points are couched and conjoined craftily together, with no small prejudice of the said Catholic religion". This was in Parsons' *Judgment of a Catholic Englishman touching the Oath of Allegiance*,[1] which covered the whole range of problems involved in the controversy. For Parsons it seemed absurd for the King to claim he was persecuting purely for civil matters when even those who had taken the oath, as Blackwell and Charnoke, were still retained in prison.[2] All Catholics are ready to take an oath which is purely civil, swearing to the King "as much loyalty as ever any Catholic subject of England did before Henry VIII or does to-day". Thus on both sides in the Oath of Allegiance controversy there are absolute but divergent criteria of what constitutes an oath which is purely civil, or mere matter of religion. The Pope claims more things under his spiritual jurisdiction than the King would allow, and the King more under his temporal jurisdiction than the Pope would allow. Between the divine right King and the divine right Pope, had there been no other parties to the controversy, liberty of conscience

[1] 1608.
[2] Parsons, *op. cit.* pp. 8–9.

218

might both ways have been extinguished, and true toleration never have been born.

Parsons remains, however, an uncompromising supporter of the rights of conscience. In *The Judgment of a Catholic Englishman* he declares that nothing is more heinous than "to force and press other men to swear against their consciences". "For he that should force a Jew or Turk to swear that there were a blessed Trinity, either knowing or suspecting that they should do it against their conscience, should sin grievously by forcing them to commit that sin."[1] It is absurd to condemn the Catholic desire for liberty of conscience as "height of pride". "For that neither breathing, nor the use of common air, is more due unto them, or common to all, than ought to be liberty of conscience to Christian men, whereby each one liveth to God, and to himself, without which we struggle with the torment of a continual lingering death."[2] In *A Discussion of the Answer of Mr William Barlow* of 1612 Parsons is even more explicit on the rights and obligations of conscience. Conscience must always be followed, and it is sin to disobey even an erroneous conscience, so long as it remains unaware of its errors.[3] To urge that conscience has no right against the command of a Prince unless it be a "good conscience accompanied with true love and faith unfeigned", is to attempt to measure the immeasurable and to give conscience no rights at all.[4] Nevertheless, Parsons justifies persecution of heretics

---

[1] *Ibid.* p. 22.   [2] *Ibid.* p. 38.
[3] Parsons, *Discussion of the Answer of Mr William Barlow*, p. 276.
[4] *Ibid.* p. 278.

by Catholics on the ground "that the Catholic Church has jus acquisitum, ancient right over heretics as her due subjects" who have become apostates,[1] and asserts that whatever the practice of Catholics, no Protestant sect has any right to refuse toleration to Catholics, because of Protestant apostasy.[2] The persecutions under Queen Mary and mediaeval kings were just and lawful, since the kings then considered their realms to be quietly settled in the ancient religion of their forefathers. But when sects "are so multiplied, as they cannot be restrained without greater scandal tumult and perturbation" they may be tolerated according to the parable of the wheat and the tares.[3] This is almost a Politique argument for toleration.

William Barclay, the leader of the English secular Catholics, defended, however, the oath, which the seculars, unlike the Jesuits and the official body of the Catholic Church, were prepared to accept. For them the oath offered a workable compromise between Pope and King. They rejected the indirect temporal power, and the power of deposition, though Barclay expresses the difficulty he is in over this matter. The Pope, he writes, is endued with a spiritual power over all kings and princes, "yet notwithstanding I am not therefore persuaded that I should alike believe, that he comprehends secular kings and princes within his temporal jurisdiction, as when they do offend against God or men, or otherwise abuse their office, he may in any sort

---

[1] Parsons, *Judgment of a Catholic Englishman*, p. 22.
[2] Parsons, *Discussion of the Answer*, pp. 250 seq.
[3] *Ibid.* p. 260.

abrogate their government and take their scepters away and bestow them on others". There are many arguments on both sides, but "for my part in regard to the zeal I bear the See Apostolic, I could wish with all my heart that it might be proved by certain and undoubted arguments that this right belongs unto it, being very ready to incline to that part to which the weightier reason and authority of truth do sway".[1] Barclay's decision in this matter was the more difficult because he believed that it was not a conflict of human and divine law (as Bellarmine asserted),[2] but of two precepts of divine law: "colere deum vera religione", and "servire atque obedire regi".

Richard Sheldon, also a Secular Catholic, in *Certain general reasons proving the lawfulness of the oath of allegiance*, repudiated more explicitly than Barclay the indirect temporal power of the Papacy, because, in some sense, there is nothing which cannot be considered as tending to edification and furthering indirectly a spiritual end. Sheldon has a sincere abhorrence of persecution. He describes the events of St Bartholomew's Eve as a "bloody massacre (horrible and detestable) nothing honourable to the Catholic cause", and remarks that had it been perpetrated "by the hands of subjects against sovereigns, heaven and earth would have cried, or poured vengeance against the authors, actors and abettors of the same". "Happy and thrice happy, would the Christian world be (though at this present most provinces are infected with one wicked

---

[1] Barclay, W., *De Potestate Papae*, p. 12.
[2] In *Responsio Mat. Torti ad librum inscriptum....*

sect or another) if all priests did and were reputed to imitate the Apostles' manner of teaching." If priests would only teach the unlawfulness of rebellion, magistrates and sovereigns would open a free passage for the truth, and happy consequences would ensue for the Catholic religion. "Perhaps persecution might last a while, but in very short time no doubt, and the blood of martyrs would bring the consciences of such sovereigns cast down and prostrate before the feet of the Lamb."[1] Sheldon was a liberal Catholic, opposed to Papal infallibility (though he considered the Church as a whole infallible) and insistent on the layman's right to refuse obedience to the Pope if he is in error. To him, as to all the Seculars, the Oath of Allegiance is a workable line of division between Church and State, though their opinions were repudiated by the great body of their Church. But it is a compromise between Pope and King not by mutual concession, but by a small section of the Church yielding to the claims of the State.

After 1615, when the Oath of Allegiance controversy had exhausted itself, the whole character of Catholic polemic changes, as indeed, did their prospects of attaining toleration. During the period of the Oath of Allegiance controversy, Catholicism was on the defensive, and there was no further prospect of any other toleration than that afforded by the Oath itself, because the personal prestige of the King as a controversialist maintaining the wholly civil nature of the Oath, was at stake. After 1615, with the commencement of the negotiations over the Spanish marriage, toleration for

[1] Sheldon, *op. cit.* p. 74.

Roman Catholics became the subject of international negotiation.[1] When these had failed the success of the High Church movement led many Catholics and Anglicans into the belief that with mutual concessions some form of reunion might be possible. In 1634, for example, Panzani, a Papal emissary, arrived in England ostensibly to settle the still persisting dispute between Seculars and Jesuits, but more especially to gain, through Henrietta Maria, some measure of toleration for Catholics. The King invested Windebank with his authority to discuss with Panzani the problem of reunion, and proposals were made on either side. Windebank was shocked to hear that the Pope censured a book by Christopher Davenport entitled *Deus, Natura, Gratia* in which the differences between Rome and Canterbury were explained away. It is true that Laud warned Charles that there would be no concessions on the Roman side, and that Charles himself was never very serious in the negotiations, merely hoping to gain concessions and Papal consent to the Oath of Allegiance. But Windebank was serious, and so was Panzani, and the very character of the negotiations is characteristic of the Catholic approach to toleration under Charles.[2] It was thus that Catholic polemic came to be occupied with the differences between the doctrine and practice of Rome and Canterbury. From the conversion of the Countess of Buckingham until the outbreak of the Civil War there were numerous conversions to and from Catholicism,

[1] The proposals of Sarmiento, which really began the negotiations, were made in July 1614. *Vide* Gardiner, *op. cit.* II, 255.

[2] Gardiner, *op. cit.* VIII, 133–8.

and need was felt for apologies on both sides. It was thus that Laud came to hold his conference with Fisher, the Jesuit, in 1622,[1] and later in the reign of Charles the whole question of the respective charity of Catholics and Protestants to each other, in withholding or conceding salvation to those of a religion other than their own, came to be controverted. Much of this literature has no relevance to the idea of toleration, but it might emerge incidentally, as we have seen it did in the controversy with Chillingworth.

[1] Gardiner, *op. cit.* IV, 281.

CHAPTER IX

CONCLUSION. THE THEORY AND
PRACTICE OF TOLERATION

THE years 1603–39 are a period of origins in the idea of religious toleration in England. There is, therefore, no large, open debate on the subject such as that which ensued upon the summoning of Parliament in 1640. Incidentally, and by implication, individuals have felt and expressed its importance, and a few explicit tracts have been devoted to its defence. But even these received, in their own age, no scrap of the attention which the historian of a later age might devote to them. The political, social and intellectual conditions of the early seventeenth century have caused the seeds of the idea to sprout in various places, but as yet they remain indigenous and isolated theories—trees of insufficient stature to influence each other's development. The work of obscure and much-hated fanatics, they were in most cases forgotten as soon as they were born. Nor did this theory, whether separatist or latitudinarian, have any appreciable effect upon immediate practice. England was to experience two revolutions and tyranny from both Parliament and the King before a measure of real toleration was secured.

In no age, however, is the idea of toleration a conception which can subsist as an end in itself. It is not simply a fragment of abstract truth which, once discovered, can be added to the sum of verified knowledge, as a piece in a jig-saw puzzle can be fitted to its proper place. For its concern is not only truth but goodness, not only human knowledge but human conduct, and although its theoretical defence presents an intellectual problem of intrinsic interest, yet it must find its end in assisting to achieve in practice that which it advocates in theory. Now those who preach the idea of toleration may, as we have seen, advocate one of two similar though not identical things. They may urge either toleration, which is a certain condition regulating the relationships between the State and the individuals and corporate bodies which constitute Society; or tolerance, which is at once a way of behaviour and an attitude of mind in the individual himself. But even tolerance and toleration are not ends in themselves. Tolerance is but a means whereby a man may find the truth in himself, and respect another view of it in others, for "a man can think no otherwise than he does". Toleration of itself solves no social problems other than those which persecution directly creates: it merely strives for certain conditions under which the problems of the age may be more advantageously solved.[1] The latitudinarians of the early seventeenth century, for example, urged tolerance not as an end in itself, but as a means which, by allowing liberty in non-fundamentals, would be the surest way to Christian unity in the few necessary fundamentals to salvation; just as the separatist tolerationist denied the use of force in religious matters to the civil power and to the bishops so that the struggle between Baptist truth

[1] Leslie Stephen, *Agnostic's Apology*: "Poisonous Opinions."

226

and Anglican error might be waged on equal terms. With these particular ends, to which the practice of tolerance and toleration are but the means, we cannot here concern ourselves, but would estimate the contribution that the idea of toleration (which includes both tolerance and toleration in its more particular sense) has to make, as an idea, to the practice of either, independently of whether those policies which it advocates are or are not being executed by those in authority. In other words, in periods of persecution does the simple preaching of the idea of toleration, even when there is not the slightest chance of authority carrying it out, help to bring practical toleration any the nearer? And can a state of toleration established be preserved in any measure by a mere theoretical exposition of its justification?

It is necessary to ask these questions because much thought on the subject to-day is conditioned by the belief that, whatever we say or think, toleration is in fact only possible in societies which are in a state of harmonious equilibrium, from which most tensions and internal conflicts have been banished; that it is the product of social change and development desirable at some periods, undesirable because impossible at others. Those who wholly accept this theory not only accept it as an account of historical fact, of which it may well be true, but accept it also as a guide to present conduct, developing a form of social fatalism which is ready to believe at any moment that the state of society makes toleration no longer possible, and is, therefore, prepared only too quickly to appeal to force to cut the gordian knot of social difficulties. In its modern form it is the theory of those who decry the importance of freedom of thought and of toleration to the magnification of freedom in its wider aspect—the freedom from the iron laws of physical and economic necessity.[1] These would sacrifice the former freedom at the slightest chance of securing the latter, because they believe that the idea of toleration, as an idea, has no contribution to make to either.

Now it is, in general, true that the possibility of religious liberty, of freedom of thought, of toleration rests, as Leslie Stephen recognized, on the state of the society in which they are to be practised. Under certain conditions of political and social stress, where, for example, a small majority is dangerously threatened by a large and menacing minority, it may be impossible for the State, representing the interests of the former, to concede any general toleration. This is not a statement of a political ideal, but an account of historical fact. The optimistic belief in the future of liberal and democratic principles which characterized so many political thinkers in the nineteenth century has suffered such rude shocks in the post-war world because it was an optimism based in part upon ignorance—ignorance of the enormous strain which the Industrial Revolution was putting upon society, and of the fact that men are much more creatures of impulse and instinct than they had been led to believe. Even Leslie Stephen, for all his recognition of the dependence of toleration upon social conditions, assumes, in his essay on "Poisonous Opinions", that no

[1] Whitehead, A. N., *Adventures of Ideas*, p. 84.

228

civilized country is likely to revert to a system of persecution in the light of human experience of its inutility. John Morley, in his essay *On Compromise*, asserted that "the right of thinking freely and acting independently, of using our minds without excessive awe of authority, and shaping our lives without unquestioning obedience to custom, is now a finally accepted principle in some sense or other with every school of thought that has the smallest chance of commanding the future". It is true that Carlyle and Matthew Arnold both appreciated the dangers of democracy, and that Bishop Creighton in the Hulsean lecture of 1894 warned his hearers that toleration was not so secure as it seemed. "I do not know", he said, "that the tolerance which is now praised by the world is very firmly established. It rests at present mainly on an equilibrium of forces that might easily be upset."[1] But the old optimism was not daunted. As late as 15 June 1914 President Wilson said to the American people: "The new things in the world are the things that are divorced from force. They are the moral compulsions of the human conscience. No man can turn away from these without turning away from the hope of all the world." Three years later the President had had reason to propound different views. In 1917 he urged the same American people to employ force as the only means of ending an intolerable world calamity, and "force without stint or limit".[2] This is the measure of the dis-

[1] Creighton, M., *Persecution and Tolerance*.
[2] Quoted by S. K. Ratcliffe, *Roots of Violence*, Merttens lecture, 1934.

illusionment and disaster which may ensue if we fail wholly to consider the social conditions of the society in which we would have toleration practised.

But although this theory may be an account of historical fact, there is no reason why it should be accepted as a whole guide to present conduct. And this for two reasons. In the first place there is nothing more deplorable than social fatalism. Much as we may believe free will ultimately to be an illusion, that there is a determined and inevitable logic in the process of history, it is no adequate reason for believing that the future can be forecast, or for denying that free will is an illusion of such intensity that compared with it most realities become pale shadows. Whether we can or cannot mould society as we would wish it, we must at least assume that we can, and never cease to urge the ideal in the hope that the logic of history may not be unfavourable to it. We are ourselves, each of us, a part of the process of history, and it is dangerous to the ideals that we cherish, to abandon tolerance and toleration at every sign of social stress with the hope that they may re-emerge eventually when the stress has purged itself by the use of force. For toleration, if it is in part the result of the solution of social problems, is just as much a condition facilitating their solution. If we cannot get true liberty without, say, Socialism, it is equally true that we cannot get Socialism without liberty. Nor is this the paradox that it seems. It merely means that we must use the methods of liberty further to enlarge and strengthen it.

In the second place, the idea of toleration has, as an

idea, much to contribute, in whatever social and political conditions, towards its own realization. The reasons given for persecution in any society have an apparent logic and are obvious to the simplest intelligence. This is true whether these reasons are tribal, the desire to avoid the vengeance of insulted deities in the forms of plague and other disasters; or political, as in societies where the gods or the supreme good in life is identified with the State or its officers; or theological, as in those societies where one faith is received as absolutely true and necessary to salvation;[1] or social, as in the theory we have just considered. To silence some one disseminating error seems the obvious way to preserve truth. Moreover, in any society there must always be those to whom persecution is not the greatest of crimes but the first of duties; as to those who believe they have an absolute and ascertained knowledge of right and truth, and that that right and truth are of such a nature that they can be achieved by force. General arguments concerning the sanctity of individual opinions as such, or of religious opinions above others, or even of the inutility of persecution are of little use here. For the theory of persecution which they oppose denies the premisses on which these arguments are founded.[2] It becomes therefore of the greatest importance that in every generation the case for liberty and toleration should be stated afresh, because the logic by which it defends itself is more subtle than the theory of persecution, and requires more judgment and intelligence in the

[1] *Vide* Sir F. Pollock, *Essays in Jurisprudence and Ethics*: "The theory of Persecution."   [2] *Ibid*.

reader. It is not merely that the theory of persecution must be encountered by a theory of toleration, but that the precise justification of toleration itself is frequently incompletely understood even by those who would declare themselves its supporters, and therefore the more easily encroached upon and diminished. Toleration is not a state or a theory which, once achieved, endures for ever like some principle of human knowledge. It is a principle which each generation has to strive for afresh, in theory as in practice, because even when secured it remains the most precarious of all human achievements. "Ceux qui diront", wrote Voltaire to the King of Prussia in 1742, "que les temps de ces crimes sont passés, qu'on ne verra plus de Barchobécas, de Mahomet, de Jean de Leyde; que les flammes des guerres de religion sont éteintes, font, ce me semble, trop d'honneur à la nature humaine. Le même poison subsiste encore, quoique moins développé; cette peste qui semble étouffé, reproduit de temps en temps des germes capables d'infecter toute la terre."[1]

In the period at present under consideration, the refutation of the theory of persecution in its seventeenth-century form, and the spreading of an understanding of the issues involved in the problem of toleration, without which in no age can toleration be achieved or secured, was the most signal practical service which the separatist tolerationist rendered to his cause. More than the latitudinarian he examined the relation of Church and State, and denied an ethical purpose to the use of force. But the latitudinarian idea of toleration had much to

[1] Quoted by Matagrin, *op. cit.* chap. v.

contribute to its practice, in a way which may be said to represent the second service of the idea of toleration, as an idea, to its practical realization. Now it has been seen that the latitudinarian tolerationist occupies himself with tolerance rather than toleration, and that his appeal is to the individual rather than the State. Tolerance, however, although in part the product of a charitable nature, is almost invariably the result of some degree of scepticism—not necessarily of complete philosophic scepticism, but certainly a scepticism about the more particular and fanatic beliefs of the age. We have seen the seventeenth-century latitudinarians reducing the essentials to salvation to what for the age were very few. It is in this scepticism that the latitudinarian idea of toleration makes its real contribution through tolerance to toleration. For scepticism, as it is the product of reason, influences immediately the conduct and behaviour of the individual, as the separatist idea of toleration cannot hope immediately to influence the State. It may, of course, be said that scepticism means indifference, and that a tolerance which thence arises is not a quality of any merit or nobility, or security. But scepticism, provided it remains an intellectual attitude, as it did in all the writers we have examined, is a necessary safeguard of the reason against a blind emotional faith which believes on authority because it cannot face intellectual uncertainty; and lends a sense of proportion and harmony to the intellectual outlook of the individual who possesses it. The faith which attaches the emotions to the rational pursuit of truth in general is no enemy of reason and of tolerance. But that faith which concerns itself with the truth instead of truth, which makes a particular conception of truth an emotional necessity apart from the evidence that has to be considered, is the seed ground of all fanaticism. It is, however, essential that that scepticism which is to assist the cause of tolerance, should remain an intellectual attitude, and not be itself subverted into an emotional conviction. In other words, scepticism must not develop into cynicism, because cynicism is merely fanaticism reversed. If the one threatens tolerance and toleration by a blind and excessive faith, the other may well deny its value altogether on no less emotional grounds. "L'incrédulité", as D'Alembert said, "est une espèce de foi pour la plupart des impies." But there is no more reason why a sceptic should be a cynic than a believer in determinism a fatalist.

The question propounded earlier in this chapter was posed in a double form because it is important to remember that the problems of toleration in the early seventeenth and in the early twentieth century are by no means identical. To-day, in England at all events, civil liberty is established. The problem is how to preserve it. In the England of the early seventeenth century the problem was how to obtain a measure of toleration from a society which regarded its practice as dangerous and sinful, and in which such thinkers who devoted themselves to the idea of toleration were giving birth to a new conception which, in the ancient world, had been unnecessary because it was universally practised, and which in the previous thousand years of Christian history would have been a heresy punishable by death.

APPENDIX

THE THEORY OF THE FAMILY
OF LOVE

The tenets of that fanatical and elusive sect called the
Family of Love are enumerated by Edmund Jessop in
A Discovery of the errors of the English Anabaptists. This
is a hostile account of the Familists, but not inaccurate:

"The most blasphemous and erronious sect this day in the
world" is "commonly called by the name of the Family of
Love, whose author was one Henrie Nicolas or H. N., for
so they will have him called: that is (as they expound it)
Homo Novus, the new man, or the holy nature or holiness,
which they make to be Christ, and sin they will have to be
anti-Christ, because it is opposite to Christ. They say that
when Adam sinned, then Christ was killed and anti-Christ
came to live. They teach that the same perfection of holiness
which Adam had before he fell is to be attained here in this
life; and affirm that all their Family of Love are as perfect
and as innocent as he. And that the resurrection of the dead
spoken of by Paul in 1 Cor. 15. and this prophecy: then
shall be fulfilled the saying which is written, O death where is
thy sting? O grave where is thy victory? is fulfilled in them
and deny all other resurrection of the body to be after this
life. They will have this blasphemer H. N. to be the Son of
God, Christ, which was to come in the end of the world to
judge the world, and say that the day of judgment is already
come; and that H. N. judgeth the world now by his doctrine",
and the Family of Love rooting out all others shall inherit
the earth. There have been "eight breakings of the light"
since Adam, and that H. N. is the "last and perfectest" by

which Christ is perfected. H. N. maketh himself God and Christ "saying that he is Godded with God, and codeified with him, and that God is homnified in him".[1]

Now in 1578 John Rogers, in *The displaying of the Family of Love*—another hostile account of their views—includes the following:

They hold that no man should be put to death for his opinion, and therefore they condemn Master Cranmer and Master Ridley for burning Joan of Kent.[2]

But in *A Supplication of the Family of Love*, which was answered in 1606, there is no mention of toleration at all. This petition is a protestation against the calumnies made against them. They deny many of these and request the King to consider the godliness of their lives, and so to release them from prison and persecution. Not only is there no mention of toleration, in a pamphlet which offered an excellent opportunity to inveigh against persecution—whether from policy or opinion—but the only reference to persecution might well be interpreted as an approval of the earlier practice of the Church towards heresy. False libels have been laid upon them "for that we, and the doctrine of H. N., might (without any indifferent trial or orderly proceeding, as heretofore hath been used in the Christian Church in such cases, for confuting and condemning of heresies) be utterly rooted out of the land".[3]

---

[1] Jessop, *op. cit.* chap. VII, p. 89.

[2] Quoted from an introductory note on the Family of Love by A. H. Bullen in an edition of Thomas Middleton's satirical play *The Family of Love*.

[3] *A Supplication of the Family of Love...Examined and found to be derogatory in a high degree to the glory of God...*, 1606, p. 47.

Toleration was never the concern of the Family of Love because they held a doctrine which enabled them largely to escape the personal problem of persecution by the practice of a mental reservation far beyond that sanctioned by the Roman Catholic Church. "They will outwardly submit to any kind of religion, and to any idolatrous service whatsoever, pretending that it is not the body that can sin but the soul." "They will profess to agree in all points with the Church of England, as also with the Church of Rome, if they should be examined by them; only this, they will not (lightly) deny their master H. N., nor speak evil of him in his writings, if they should be put to it, and there is no other way than this to discover them."[1]

[1] Jessop, *op. cit.* pp. 90–1.

INDEX

239

INDEX

INDEX